Mothers' Wit

First published in 2006

This edition published 2007 by
Sevenoaks
an imprint of the
Carlton Publishing Group
20 Mortimer Street
London W1T 3JW

2 4 6 8 10 9 7 5 3

A catalogue record for this book is available from
the British Library

ISBN 978-1-86200-452-8

Printed in Great Britain
by Mackays

Mothers' Wit

Humorous Quotes on Mums and Motherhood

Allison Vale
and
Alison Rattle

SEVENOAKS

To Mum, of course, love you millions!

(Thanks to Draycott and Rodney Stoke F.S.)

A.R.

To the best Mum in the world … mine.

A.V.

Contents

Introduction

The dictionary definition of the word 'mother' is 'A female who has given birth to offspring.' A truism, yet woefully incomplete. To be a mother is a woman's greatest vocation in life, for mothers make the world go round – literally.

The word mother is linked intrinsically to images of babbling babes in arms, wind-fresh laundry, steamy kitchens, the smell of Dettol, the taste of toffee, the feel of a warm, soft bosom and the touch of deft hands which create, nurture and protect.

How many women spent many a tortured hour in adolescent years, longing for the glory of curing cancer, the fame of the movie star, the adulation of the music industry or the giddy heights of academic brilliance? How many set out to achieve the luminosity of stardom in the first unsteady steps into adulthood? By their thirties, how many more have discovered instead the intensity of their child's first steps across the living room and into their arms?

You set out wanting the world to worship the ground you walk on and pretty soon you realize that motherhood brings with it your own little world that will do exactly that … At least until that little world grows into spotty, hairy and misunderstood adolescence; all pop stars and pop tarts and black hair dye. (At this point you may find yourself wondering what was so bad about the curing cancer idea after all … and so nature turns full circle.)

It's tempting to see motherhood as an art – and one that we have only just begun to grasp in recent times. Medieval motherhood was simply a question of mating, gestating and liberating, followed by an extended period of breastfeeding. Wasn't it?

Teachers asked in the 1940s to comment on the most serious disciplinary issues they faced on a regular basis listed litter and untucked shirts as top gripes. Imagine that. Today's teachers, asked the same question, list violent crime, suicide, drug and alcohol abuse as theirs. So what – or whom – is to blame?

Today's mother faces an overwhelming barrage of advice. Education, Western wealth and technological advances mean that a woman is faced with gargantuan choices to make about every issue from conception on. The path she chooses to take on her child's dad, diet, diapers and dance class is analysed and, inevitably, criticized. However carefully she makes these decisions, if she listens long enough, someone, somewhere, will be bitching.

The truth, for those wanting to discover it, is that motherhood has never been easy: toddlers have always been trouble; teenagers have always been foul; mothers-in-law have always been judgemental and dreaded.

Mothers' Wit

This collection of mothers' wit delves into the heart of motherhood, the joys of which include catching a child's vomit in your hands and cleavage in an attempt to save the carpet, to the more serene moments of guiltily lapping up daytime telly while breastfeeding a newborn.

A mother lies at the heart of every person and we track her development from single woman searching for a potential mate to the white-haired matriarch doling out nuggets of wisdom. We don't attempt to glorify the mother – after all, no mum is perfect and some are far from it. Instead, we capture a mother's foibles, from hatred of housework and ineptitude in the kitchen, to dealing with discipline and the guilt of going out to work. Of course there are sprinklings of the soppy and sentimental too, as we cannot help but love our mums!

Here, the combined wit and wisdom of great characters in history, from Pliny to Presley, Nietzsche to Nigella, the Marquis de Sade to Dame Edna, testify to the emotional minefield that is motherhood. A mother's influence has moulded the most powerful people on earth and even prompted presidents to form lifelong opinions on broccoli.

Motherhood is ...

... [feeling] like an acrobat high above a crowd out of which my own parents, my in-laws, potential employers, phantoms of 'other women who do it' and a thousand faceless eyes stare up.

... a ticker tape parade for two

... knowing when to be the wind in your child's sails and when to calm the waters.

... never refusing their home-made cakes.

... an all-terrain vehicle.

... never robbing your child of the opportunity to make a bad choice all on his own.

... only ever walking away from them to check that their coast is clear.

... always being there when they've popped all their bubble wrap.

... laughing at their jokes though they are not very funny and listening to their problems though they are not very serious.

... spending half your time worrying how they will turn out and the other half wondering when they will turn in.

... like living with a bowling alley in the brain.

... only having time to shave one leg.

... spending longer on the toilet because its feels good to be alone.

... catching your kid's sick.

... enjoying your meal even though someone else's kid is throwing up.

... refusing to let him have toy weapons, while he nibbles on a sandwich till it looks like a gun.

... counting ketchup as one of their daily five portions of fruit and veg.

... cutting your husband's garlic bread up into manageable portions at the restaurant.

... realizing at least halfway home from nursery that you are still singing along to their 'Wheels on the Bus' song tape.

... going back to work for the rest.

... a glorious career!

... the best all round job. No other career would allow you to be plumber, drill sergeant, nurse, chef, umpire, banker, telephonist and international diplomat – all before 9.30 a.m.

All Anon.

... having someone else to blame when there is a rude smell in the air.

Jane Horrocks

... never being number one in your list of priorities and not minding at all.

Jasmine Guinness

... mind-blowing.

Britney Spears

... the biggest on-the-job training scheme in the world.

Erma Bombeck

... the first word that occurs to politicians and columnists and popes when they raise the question, 'Why isn't life turning out the way we want it?'

Mary Kay Blakely

... perhaps the only unpaid position where failure to show up can result in arrest.

Mary Kay Blakely

… the great divide between one's own childhood and adulthood. All at once someone is totally dependent upon you. You are no longer the child of your mother but the mother of your child.

Elaine Heffner

… a wonderful thing. What a pity to waste it on the children.

Judith Pugh

… the keystone of the arch of matrimonial happiness.

Thomas Jefferson

The story of a mother's life: Trapped between a scream and a hug.

Cathy Guisewite

… like Albania – you can't trust the brochures, you have to go there.

Marni Jackson

… not for the faint-hearted. Frogs, skinned knees and the insults of teenage girls are not meant for the wimpy.

Danielle Steel

… nothing more than feeding the hand that bites you.

Ann Diehl

The Best of Times, the Worst of Times

Nothing will ever make you as happy or sad, as proud or as tired as motherhood.

Elia Parsons

There is a widespread feeling that we have to do it all alone, and if we don't know something, or can't manage it, or, heaven forbid, don't want to, there is something lacking in our makeup.

Sally Placksin

Sometimes the laughter in mothering is the recognition of the ironies and absurdities. Sometimes, though, it's just pure, unthinking delight.

Barbara Schapiro

Sometimes the strength of motherhood is greater than natural laws.

Barbara Kingsolver

There never was a child so lovely, but his mother was glad to get him asleep.

Ralph Waldo Emerson

Be nice to your children, for they will choose your rest home.

Phyllis Diller

It is not until you become a mother that your judgement slowly turns to compassion and understanding.

Erma Bombeck

It will be gone before you know it. The fingerprints on the wall appear higher and higher. Then suddenly they disappear.

Dorothy Evslin

Over the years I have learned that motherhood is much like an austere religious order, the joining of which obligates one to relinquish all claims to personal possessions.

Nancy Stahl

The art of making a mistake is crucial to motherhood. To be effective and gain the respect she needs to function, a mother must have her children believe she has never engaged in sex, never made a bad decision, never caused her own mother a moment's anxiety, and was never a child.

Erma Bombeck

The joys of motherhood are never fully experienced until the children are in bed.

Anon.

When I pick up one of my children and cuddle them, all the strain and stress of life temporarily disappears. There is nothing more wonderful than motherhood and no one will ever love you as much as a small child.

Nicola Horlick

You don't at last arrive at being a parent and suddenly feel satisfied and joyful. It is a constantly reopening adventure.

Anon.

Is there indeed anything more terrible, more criminal, than our glorified sacred function of motherhood?

Emma Goldman

Hence the spiritual weariness of the conscientious mother: you're always finding out just one more vital tidbit.

Sonia Taitz

All my life I've felt like somebody's wife, or somebody's mother or somebody's daughter. Even all the time we were together, I never knew who I was. And that's why I had to go away.

Joanna Kramer, Kramer vs Kramer

'It's hard enough to adjust [to the lack of control] in the beginning,' says a corporate vice president and single mother. 'But then you realize that everything keeps changing, so you never regain control.'

Anne C. Weisberg and Carol A. Buckler

There's always room for improvement, you know – it's the biggest room in the house.

Louise Heath Leber

I think motherhood makes you apathetic because you're always so tired. I don't know how anyone can march or be politically active when they've only had three hours' sleep.

Jo Brand

For a parent, it's hard to recognize the significance of your work when you're immersed in the mundane details. Few of us, as we run the bathwater or spread the peanut butter on the bread, proclaim proudly, 'I'm making my contribution to the future of the planet.'

Joyce Maynard

You cannot even simply become a mother any more. You must choose motherhood.

Eleanor Holmes Norton

I remember opening the refrigerator late one night and finding [I had chilled] a roll of aluminium foil next to a pair of small red tennis shoes ... I quickly closed the door and ran upstairs to make sure I had put the babies in their cribs instead of the linen closet.

Mary Kay Blakely

Suddenly we have a baby who poops and cries, and we are trying to calm, clean up, and pin things together all at once. Then as fast as we learn to cope – so soon – it is hard to recall why diapers ever seemed so important. The frontiers change, and now perhaps we have a teenager we can't reach.

Polly Berrien Berends

What Makes a Mother?

… snuggly buggly stuff.

Riley, aged 7

… laughter and silliness.

Anna, aged 26¾

… God and sweets.

Tom, aged 9

… brown sugar.

Ella, aged 10

… another mum.

Daisy, aged 12

… smiles and cookies.

Louisa, aged 6

A woman has two smiles that an angel might envy, the smile that accepts a lover before words are uttered, and the smile that lights on the first-born babe, and assures it of a mother's love.

Thomas C. Haliburton

If evolution really works how come mothers only have two hands?

Ed Dussault

Women's courage is rather different from men's. The fact that women have to bring up children and look after husbands makes them braver at facing long-term issues, such as illness. Men are more immediately courageous.

Mary Wesley

Simply having children does not make mothers.

John A. Shed

A mother understands what a child does not say.

Anon.

I will fight for my children on any level so they can reach their potential as human beings and in their public duties.

Princess Diana

A true mother knows that when their child pampers them with compliments, they really just want something.

Kirsten, a mother

The heart of a mother is a deep abyss at the bottom of which you will always find forgiveness.

Honoré de Balzac

A mother is the truest friend we have, when trials heavy and sudden, fall upon us … [she will] endeavour by her kind precepts and counsels to dissipate the clouds of darkness, and cause peace to return to our hearts.

Washington Irving

What Makes a Mother?

There's a lot more to being a woman than being a mother, but there's a lot more to being a mother than most people suspect.

Roseanne Barr

A mother is not a person to lean on but a person to make leaning unnecessary.

Dorothy Fisher

A mother's arms are made of tenderness and children sleep soundly in them.

Victor Hugo

The patience of a mother might be likened to a tube of toothpaste – it's never quite all gone.

Anon.

There is no way to be a perfect mother, and a million ways to be a good one.

Jill Churchill

The trouble with mothers is that however well groomed and sophisticated you appear to strangers, they know your knickers are probably held up with a safety pin.

Samantha Armstrong

Biology is the least of what makes someone a mother.

Oprah Winfrey

Mothers' love is peace. It need not be acquired, it need not be deserved.

Erich Fromm

Mothers' Wit

A mother who is really a mother is never free.

Honoré de Balzac

You never realize how much your mother loves you till you explore the attic – and find every letter you ever sent her, every finger painting, clay pot, bead necklace, Easter chicken, cardboard Santa Claus, paperlace Mother's Day card and school report since day one.

Pam Brown

Mother: The most beautiful word on the lips of mankind.

Kahlil Gibran

Most mothers are instinctive philosophers.

Harriet Beecher Stowe

It is never easy being a mother. If it were easy fathers would do it.

Anon.

The hand that rocks the cradle is the hand that rules the world.

William Ross Wallace

If a woman has to choose between catching a fly ball and saving an infant's life, she will choose to save the infant's life without even considering if there are men on base.

Dave Barry

What the mother sings to the cradle goes all the way down to the coffin.

Henry Ward Beecher

What Makes a Mother?

A mother is a mother still,
The holiest thing alive.

Samuel Taylor Coleridge

A mother is she who can take the place of all others, but whose place no one else can take.

Cardinal Mermillod

A Freudian slip is when you say one thing but mean a mother.

Anon.

Everybody knows that a good mother gives her children a feeling of trust and stability … Somehow even her clothes feel different to her children's hands from anybody else's clothes. Only to touch her skirt or her sleeve makes a troubled child feel better.

Katharine Butler Hathaway

Mothers are a biological necessity; fathers are a social invention.

Margaret Mead

Mother is the dead heart of the family, spending father's earnings on consumer goods to enhance the environment in which he eats, sleeps and watches the television.

Germaine Greer

The ideal mother, like the ideal marriage, is a fiction.

Milton R. Sapirstein

Mothers' Wit

We really have no definition of mother in our law books. Mother was believed to have been so basic that no definition was deemed necessary.

Marianne O. Battani

A mother is a woman with a twenty-five-hour day who can still find time to play with her family.

Iris Peck

She discovered with great delight that one does not love one's children just because they are one's children but because of the friendship formed while raising them.

Gabrel García Márquez

In particular, the State recognizes that by her life within the home, woman gives to the State a support without which the common good cannot be achieved.

The Irish Constitution

To get the whole world out of bed
And washed, and dressed, and warmed, and fed,
To work, and back to bed again,
Believe me, Saul, costs worlds of pain.

John Masefield

Mothers are the only race of people that speak the same tongue. A mother in Manchuria could converse with a mother in Nebraska and never miss a word.

Will Rogers

A mother is like a teabag – you never know how strong she is until she gets in hot water.

Anon.

What Makes a Mother?

A mother is someone who dreams great dreams for you, but then she lets you chase the dreams you have for yourself and loves you just the same.

Anon.

That dear octopus from whose tentacles we never quite escape, nor in our innermost hearts never quite wish to.

Dodie Smith

It is really too much of a woman to expect her to bring up her husband and her children too.

Lilian Bell

All that remains to the mother in modern consumer society is the role of scapegoat; psychoanalysis uses huge amounts of money and time to persuade analysands to foist their problems on to the absent mother.

Germaine Greer

The greatest love is a mother's; then comes a dog's, then comes a sweetheart's.

Polish proverb

If Heaven decides to rain or your mother to remarry, there is no way to stop either.

Chinese proverb

I would rather be the child of a mother who has all the inner conflicts of the human being than be mothered by someone for whom all is easy and smooth, who knows all the answers, and is a stranger to doubt.

D. W. Winnicott

We say that a girl with her doll anticipates the mother. It is more true, perhaps, that most mothers are still but children with playthings.

F. H. Bradley

Whether our relationship is strained or easy, hostile or amiable, we need [our mother] if only in memory or fantasy, to conjugate our history, validate our femaleness, and guide our way.

Victoria Secunda

A mother is like a pavement in the middle of the fast lane.

Anon.

To me, the black black woman is our essential mother – the blacker she is the more us she is – and to see the hatred that is turned on her is enough to make me despair, almost entirely, of our future as a people.

Alice Walker

Your mother is like your bra: close to your heart and there for support.

Anon.

The Americans are violently oral ... That's why in America the mother is all-important and the father has no position at all – isn't respected in the least. Even the American passion for laxatives can be explained as an oral manifestation. They want to get rid of any unpleasantness taken in through the mouth.

W. H. Auden

What Makes a Mother?

A mother makes all life's worries smaller – except for the phone bill.

Anon.

Fortunately for those who pay their court through such foibles, a fond mother, though, in pursuit of praise for her children, the most rapacious of human beings, is likewise the most credulous; her demands are exorbitant; but she will swallow any thing.

Jane Austen

Feeling needy – mistaking vulnerability for weakness – doesn't fit in with our image of what being a mother is all about.

Sally Placksin

A mother's love, in a degree, sanctifies the most worthless offspring.

Hosea Ballou

A mother is the only person on earth who can divide her love among ten children and each child still have all her love.

Anon.

The woman is the home. That's where she used to be, and that's where she still is. You might ask me, 'What if a man tries to be part of the home – will the woman let him?' I answer yes. Because then he becomes one of the children.

Marguerite Duras

My mother hatched my chickens even before I had time to count them.

Anon.

The kind of power mothers have is enormous. Take the skyline of Istanbul – enormous breasts, pathetic little willies, a final revenge on Islam. I was so scared I had to crouch in the bottom of the boat when I saw it.

Angela Carter

When I Became a Mother I Learned That ...

... punching your sister in the face can happen accidentally.

... stretch marks last for ever.

... hamsters are more resilient than they look.

... the leading brand of washing powder does not remove *all* stains.

... as soon as you pass the last motorway station for ninety miles, someone will need the loo.

... I don't have to use a road map – I can just use the veins on my legs.

... an Oscar is never more deserved than by a child just asked to clean her room.

... it's no good crying over spilled baby cereal on a wicker chair.

… bags under the eyes do not disappear until three years after your last child leaves home.

… mothers alone hold the secret recipe for refilling ice-cube trays.

… valuable pieces of artwork don't cost a penny.

All anon.

The Vetting Process

Whenever I date a guy, I think, is this the man I want my kids to spend their weekends with?

Rita Rudner

A girl can wait for the right man to come along, but in the meantime that still doesn't mean she can't have a wonderful time with all the wrong ones.

Cher

If you never want to see a man again, say, 'I love you. I want to marry you. I want to have children' – they leave skid marks.

Rita Rudner

Nowadays, people live together. If it doesn't work they part, one hopes without acrimony. They marry when they want to have children. There's no stigma. There's no vocabulary either. I don't like the word 'partner', it makes me think of a law firm. I like the word 'lover'.

Mary Wesley

Mothers' Wit

Never marry a man who hates his mother, because he'll end up hating you.

Jill Bennett

I married the first man I ever kissed. When I tell this to my children they just about throw up.

Barbara Bush

I am fed up with men who use sex like a sleeping pill.

Toni Braxton

If someone had told me years ago that sharing a sense of humour was so vital to partnerships, I could have avoided a lot of sex!

Kate Beckinsale

Personally, I think if a woman hasn't met the right man by the time she's 24, she may be lucky.

Deborah Kerr

When I eventually met Mr Right I had no idea that his first name was Always.

Rita Rudner

She's descended from a long line her mother listened to.

Gypsy Rose Lee

The first time you buy a house you see how pretty the paint is and buy it. The second time you look to see if the basement has termites. It's the same with men.

Lupe Velez

I'm trying to find a man to share my life with, but it's not been easy. I'm a 35-year-old woman with two small children.

Nicole Kidman

This 'relationship' business is one big waste of time. It is just Mother Nature urging you to breed, breed, breed. Learn from nature. Learn from our friend the spider. Just mate once and then kill him.

Ruby Wax

Find a nice man, marry him, have babies and shut up.

Wauhillau La Hay

You know what we can be like: see a guy and think he's cute one minute, the next minute our brains have us married with kids, the following minute we see him having an extramarital affair. By the time someone says, 'I'd like you to meet Cecil,' we shout, 'You're late again with the child support.'

Cynthia Heimel

Surely there must be some way to find a husband, or, for that matter, merely an escort, without sacrificing one's privacy, self-respect, and interior decorating scheme. For example men could be imported from developing countries.

Barbara Ehrenreich

Before I met my husband I'd never fallen in love, though I'd stepped in it a few times.

Rita Rudner

Marrying a man is like buying something you've been admiring for a long time in a shop window. You may love it when you get it home, but it doesn't always go with everything else in the house.

Jean Kerr

I require three things in a man. He must be handsome, ruthless and stupid.

Dorothy Parker

These are times not to flirt. When you're sick. When you're with children. When you're on the witness stand.

Joyce Jilson

If you want to stay single … look for the perfect mate.

Anon.

The women of my mother's generation had, in the main, only one decision to make about their lives: whom they would marry … There were roles and there were rules.

Anna Quindlen

The trouble with some women is they get all excited about nothing – and then they marry him.

Cher

Whatever you may look like, marry a man your own age – as your beauty fades, so will his eyesight.

Phyllis Diller

A man on a date wonders if he'll get lucky. The woman already knows.

Monica Piper

I think men who have a pierced ear are better prepared for marriage. They've experienced pain and bought jewellery.

Rita Rudner

I don't deny that an odd man here and there, if he's caught young and trained up proper, and if his mother has spanked him well beforehand, may turn out a decent being.

Lucy Maud Montgomery

Bigamy is having one husband too many. Monogomy is the same.

Erica Jong

I've been married three times, and each time I married the right person.

Margaret Mead

A good marriage is at least 80 per cent good luck in finding the right person at the right time. The rest is trust.

Nanette Newman

A bride at her second marriage does not wear a veil. She wants to see what she is getting.

Helen Rowland

Is it better for a woman to marry a man who loves her than a man she loves?

Anon.

A good place to meet men is at the dry cleaners. These men have jobs and usually bathe.

Rita Rudner

Men should be like Kleenex, soft, strong and disposable.

Cher

LAWYER: 'How did you happen to go to Dr Cherney?'
WITNESS: 'Well, a gal down the road had had several of her children by Dr Cherney and said he was really good.

Genuine courtroom transcript

It's slim pickings out there. When you're first single, you're so optimistic. At the beginning you're like: I want to meet a guy who's really smart, really sweet, really good-looking, has a really great career … Six months later, you're like: Lord – any mammal with a day job!

Carol Leifer

A young man asked me: 'What in your opinion is the ideal husband?' I cast about hastily in my mind and then replied, 'Why – no husband at all.'

Gertrude Atherton

If a man prepares dinner for you and the salad contains three or more types of lettuce, he is serious.

Rita Rudner

Don't call him and rarely return his calls.

Ellen Fein and Sherrie Schneider

Feeling Broody?

Making the decision to have a child is momentous. It is to decide for ever to have your heart go walking around outside your body.

Elizabeth Stone

They assume that I want a boyfriend, and yeah, that I'd probably like to have a baby and get married – but they're wrong.

Amy Sedaris

Women need not always keep their mouths shut and their wombs open.

Emma Goldman

Many children, many cares; no children, no felicity.

Christian Nestell Bovee

We in the West do not refrain from childbirth because we are concerned about the population explosion or because we feel we cannot afford children, but because we do not like children.

Germaine Greer

My husband and I are either going to buy a dog or have a child. We can't decide whether to ruin our carpet or ruin our lives.

Rita Rudner

It would seem that something which means poverty, disorder and violence every single day should be avoided entirely, but the desire to beget children is a natural urge.

Phyllis Diller

There comes a time when a woman needs to stop focusing on her looks and focus her energies on raising her children. This time comes at the moment of conception. A child needs a role model, not a super model.

Astrid Alauda

Our bodies are shaped to bear children, and our lives are a working out of the processes of creation. All our ambitions and intelligence are beside that great elemental point.

Saint Augustine

At the age of 16, I was already dreaming of having a baby because I felt myself to be an adult, but my mum forbade it. Right now, I feel like a teenager and I want to have fun for one or two more years before starting a family.

Milla Jovovich

Now the thing about having a baby – and I can't be the first person to have noticed this – is that thereafter you have it.

Jean Kerr

The best thing that could happen to motherhood already has. Fewer women are going into it.

Victoria Billings

It was palpable, all that wanting: mother wanting something more, dad wanting something more, everyone wanting something more. This wasn't going to do for us fifties girls; we were going to have to change the equation even if it meant … abstaining from motherhood, because clearly that was where mother got caught.

Anne Taylor Fleming

Of all the rights of woman, the greatest is to be a mother.

Lyn Yutang

I am so ready to be a mommy. I can't wait! I notice every little baby dress, every little baby toy, every little baby thing.

Halle Berry

I've got a checklist of things I want – including a Brit, a Grammy, an Oscar and a white poodle. Sometimes it gets lonely, and I want a baby too! I'm ticking things off the list.

Joss Stone

I want to have children and I know my time is running out. I want to have them while my parents are still young enough to take care of them.

Rita Rudner

Being a housewife and mother is the biggest job in the world, but if it doesn't interest you don't do it – I would have made a terrible mother.

Katharine Hepburn

Having children is what a woman is born for really.

Nastassia Kinski

The role of a mother is the role of a lifetime. Just give me my paycheck, help me find a husband and let me raise a family.

Moira Kelly

The one point on which all women are in furious secret rebellion against the existing law is the saddling of the right to a child with the obligation to become the servant of a man.

George Bernard Shaw

Women now have choices. They can be married, not married, have a job, not have a job, be married with children, unmarried with children. Men have the same choice we've always had: work or prison.

Tim Allen

I never used to like babies. I mean, I'd always think, 'Well, if a baby were more like a chimpanzee, I'd have one.'

Candice Bergen

I am scared of becoming a mother.

Liv Tyler

It was always the work that was the gyroscope in my life. I don't know who could have lived with me. As an architect you're absolutely devoured. A woman's cast in a lot of roles and a man isn't. I couldn't be an architect and be a wife and mother.

Eleanore Kendall Pettersen

Instead of needing lots of children we need high-quality children.

Margaret Mead

I think I'm going into retirement. Any more babies coming from me are going to be keepers.

Shannon Boff, 23-year-old surrogate mother

Do not breed. Nothing gives less pleasure than childbearing. Pregnancies are damaging to health, spoil the figure, wither the charms, and it's the cloud of uncertainty for ever hanging over these events that darkens a husband's mood.

Marquis de Sade

I'll probably never have children because I don't believe in touching people for any reason.

Paula Poundstone

Being single is better … for the simple reason that I wouldn't want to change no diapers. Of course, if I did get married, I'd figure something out. I'd just phone my mother and have her come over for some coffee and diaper-changing.

Kirsten, aged 10

The compelled mother loves her child as the caged bird sings. The song does not justify the cage nor the love the enforcement.

Germaine Greer

Sexual liberation, as a slogan, turns out to be another kind of bondage. For a woman it offers orgasm as her ultimate and major fulfilment; it's better than motherhood.

Victoria Billings

No matter how lonely you get or how many birth announcements you receive, the trick is not to get frightened. There's nothing wrong with being alone.

Wendy Wasserstein

We've begun to long for the pitter patter of little feet. So we bought a dog. Well, it's cheaper and you get more feet.

Rita Rudner

I get those maternal feelings. Like when I'm lying on the couch and can't reach the remote. 'Boy, a kid would be nice, right now.'

Kathleen Madigan

Biological possibility and desire are not the same as biological need. Women have childbearing equipment. For them to choose not to use the equipment is no more blocking what is instinctive than it is for a man who, muscles or no, chooses not to be a weightlifter.

Betty Rollin

I think I'd be a good mother. Maybe a little overprotective. Like I would never let the kid out – of my body.

Wendy Liebman

Baby Making

Women who miscalculate are called mothers.

Abigail Van Buren

My ultimate fantasy is to entice a man to my bedroom, put a gun to his head and say, 'Make babies or die.'

Ruby Wax

[He considers me] just a uterus with legs.

Mary Beth Whitehead, describing a Superior Court judge's ruling that she could not keep the child she had conceived as a surrogate mother

I like trying to get pregnant. I'm not so sure about childbirth.

George Eliot

My father was a simple man. My mother was a simple woman. You see the result standing in front of you, a simpleton.

Chic Murray

Those of you who have the talent to do honour to poor womanhood, have all given yourselves over to babymaking.

Susan B. Anthony

We thought it might be fun to have twins.

Sam Frustaci, explaining why his wife chose to take fertility pills and her subsequent delivery of septuplets

As soon as my husband and I can be in the same city, at the same time, I'd say we have a better chance of actually having children.

Sarah Jessica Parker

If it's so hard to get pregnant, how do you account for the number of crying children on planes?

Samantha, Sex in the City

I've tried several varieties of sex. The conventional position makes me claustrophobic and the others give me a stiff neck or lockjaw.

Tallulah Bankhead

Most of sex is psychological – most of it is between our ears and not between our legs.

Joy Browne

When all is said and done, monotony may after all be the best condition for creation.

Margaret Sackville

He only has one ball and I have a lazy ovary. In what world does that create a baby … It's like the special Olympics of conception.

Miranda, Sex in the City

A period isn't a full stop. It's a new beginning. I don't mean all that creativity, life-giving force, earth-mother stuff, I mean it's a new beginning to the month, relief that you're not pregnant, when you don't have to have a child.

Michelene Wandor

Mom + Dad + beer = Me

Toilet graffito

The idea that population growth guarantees a better life – financially or otherwise – is a myth that only those who sell diapers, baby carriages and the like have any right to believe.

Anon.

Abortion is a skilfully marketed product sold to women at a crisis time in their life. If the product is defective, she can't return it for a refund.

Carol Everett

It is said that life begins when the foetus can exist apart from its mother. By this definition, many people in Hollywood are legally dead.

Jay Leno

I'm not pregnant! It's a miracle! I shagged and shagged and shagged and all the little bastards missed!

Jane, Coupling

Mom … I'm pregnant. I went out with a guy I hardly knew, we had sex for *hours* and I got pregnant. And I'm not gonna marry him! [chuckles] I'm keeping the baby and if it's a girl, I'm naming it Gidget.

Jackie, Roseanne

Well the pregnancy test said I'm not pregnant: the hamster didn't turn blue.

Alice, Vicar of Dibley

A Bumpy Ride Pregnancy

GIRL: Mother, I'm pregnant.
MOTHER: Are you sure it's yours?

Anon.

… she said, 'Do you mind if I sit down, 'cos I'm pregnant?' I said, 'You don't look it, how long have you been pregnant?' She said, 'Only ten minutes, but doesn't it make you feel tired.'

Max Miller

Think of stretch marks as pregnancy service stripes.

Joyce Armor

By far the most common craving of pregnant women is not to be pregnant.

Phyllis Diller

… it's possible that a pregnant woman who scrubs her house from floor to ceiling [just before her baby is born] is responding to a biological imperative … Of course there are those who believe that … the burst of energy that propels a pregnant woman to clean her house is a perfectly natural response to their mother's impending visit.

Mary Arrigo

Life is tough enough without having someone kick you from the inside.

Rita Rudner

If men were equally at risk from this condition … then I am sure that pregnancy would be classified as a sexually transmitted disease and abortions would be no more controversial than emergency appendectomies.

Barbara Ehrenreich

If pregnancy were a book they would cut the last two chapters.

Nora Ephron

Never go to your high school reunion pregnant or they will think that is all you have done since you graduated.

Erma Bombeck

Women are nothing but machines for producing children.

Napoleon Bonaparte

You should never say anything to a woman that even remotely suggests that you think she's pregnant unless you can see an actual baby emerging from her at that moment.

Dave Barry

It takes nine months to have a baby no matter how many people you put on the job.

American proverb

I positively think that ladies who are always *enceinte* quite disgusting; it is more like a rabbit or a guinea pig than anything else and really it is not very nice.

Queen Victoria

Most of a modest woman's life was spent, after all, in denying what, in one day at least of every year, was made obvious.

Virginia Woolf

Being slightly paranoid is like being slightly pregnant – it tends to get worse.

Molly Irvins

Everything to do with women is a mystery, and everything to do with women has one solution: it's called pregnancy.

Friedrich Nietzsche

A gorgeous example of denial is the story about the little girl who was notified that a baby brother or sister was on the way. She listened in thoughtful silence, then raised her gaze from her mother's belly to her eyes and said, 'Yes, but who will be the new baby's mommy?'

Judith Viorst

I've got a really big baby growing out of my stomach and, quite frankly, it looks like I've got one growing out of my bottom too.

Fay Ripley

You do a lot of growing up when you're pregnant. It's suddenly like, 'Yikes. Here it is, folks. Playtime is over.'

Connie Fioretto

Being pregnant is an occupational hazard of being a wife.

Queen Victoria

I've begun to love this little creature and to anticipate his birth as a fresh twist to a knot which I do not wish to untie.

Mary Wollestonecraft Shelley

Next up: the Clue Pregnancy Test. If the square turns pink, you've got one!

Sarah Trombley

If I had my life to live over, instead of wishing away nine months of pregnancy, I'd have cherished every moment and realized that the wonderment growing inside me was the only chance in life to assist God in a miracle.

Erma Bombeck

Pregnancy represents one of the great unknowns in life. Everyone's at least a little worried about how it will turn out.

Lawrence Kutner

Her girlfriends asked that innocent, 'What? What appeals to you?' when her pregnancy cravings appeared. Her gaze merely fell on her husband.

H. Stavhana

It's like being grounded for eighteen years.

Poster warning against teen pregnancy

The frequency of personal questions grows in direct proportion to your increasing girth … No matter how much you wish for privacy, your pregnancy is a public event to which everyone feels invited.

Jean Marzollo

Pregnancy is not a disease. It is the ultimate manifestation of health.

Laura Shanley

I was four months pregnant with my fourth child and one evening my husband decided to tell our three children the news while I was at work. 'Mummy is having a baby,' he said. Stephanie, my 8-year-old, asked, 'Does she know?'

Tania, a mother

Although they tell you you are most beautiful when you're pregnant, all the models who epitomize beauty have skinny waistlines. So they're shitting you right from the start.

Florynce R. Kennedy

A man did this to me, Oprah.

T-shirt worn by pregnant woman

I think the baby kicked, oh no wait, oh no, it's the elastic in my underwear busted.

Phoebe, Friends

I was horrified to find myself being referred to as a geriatric mother who, by the time my child had reached school age, would have a brain like a soggy rusk and would have the personality and mobility of a stuffed parrot.

Jan Anderson, on pregnancy in her forties

This morning I threw up at a board meeting. I was sure the cat was out of the bag, but no one seemed to think anything about it; apparently it's quite common for people to throw up at board meetings.

Jane Wagner

The only time a woman wishes she were a year older is when she is expecting a baby.

Mary Marsh

Advice to expectant mothers: you must remember that when you are pregnant, you are eating for two. But you must also remember that the other one of you is about the size of a golf ball, so let's not go overboard with it. I mean a lot of pregnant women eat as though the other person they're eating for is Orson Welles.

Dave Barry

Labour Intensive

Delivery is the wrong word to describe the childbearing process. Delivery is, 'Here's your pizza.' Takes thirty minutes or less. Exorcism, I think, is more apt: 'Please! Get the hell out of my body!'

Jeff Stilson

Giving birth is like taking your lower lip and forcing it over your head.

Carole Burnett

My obstetrician was so dumb that when I gave birth he forgot to cut the cord. For a year that kid followed me everywhere. It was like having a dog on a leash.

Joan Rivers

I realize why women die in childbirth – it's preferable.

Sherry Glaser

Mothers' Wit

Somewhere on this globe, every ten seconds, there is a woman giving birth to a child. She must be found and stopped.

Sam Levenson

A suburban mother's role is to deliver children obstetrically once, and by car for ever after.

Peter De Vries

The moment a child is born, the mother is also born. She never existed before. The woman existed, but the mother, never. A mother is something absolutely new.

Rajneesh

Don't tell your kids you had an easy birth or they won't respect you. For years I used to wake up my daughter and say, 'Melissa, you ripped me to shreds. Now go back to sleep.'

Joan Rivers

I want to have children, but my friends scare me. One of my friends told me she was in labour for thirty-six hours. I don't even want to do anything that feels good for thirty-six hours.

Rita Rudner

I once heard two ladies going on and on about the pains of childbirth and how men don't seem to know what real pain is. I asked if either of them ever got themselves caught in a zipper.

Emo Philips

Is it true when you were born the doctor turned around and slapped your mother?

Tick, Adventures of Priscilla, Queen of the Desert

Watching a baby being born is a little like watching a wet St Bernard coming in through the cat door.

Jeff Foxworthy

If we mums can push nine-pound babies through our bodies, some of them with heads as big as bowling balls, surely we can push legislation through the halls of Congress.

Donna Dees-Thomases

Poverty is a lot like childbirth – you know it is going to hurt before it happens, but you'll never know how much until you experience it.

Joanne Kathleen Rowling

Childbirth is no more a miracle than eating food and a turd coming out of your ass.

Bill Hicks

Giving birth is not a matter of pushing, expelling the baby, but of yielding, surrendering to birth energy.

Marie Reid

Anyone who thinks women are the weaker sex never witnessed childbirth.

Anon.

The world doesn't want to hear the labour pains, they just want to see the baby.

Anon.

Mothers' Wit

My husband was just OK-looking. I was in labour and I said to him, 'What if she's ugly? You're ugly!'

Beverly Johnson

When I was born I was so surprised I didn't talk for a year and a half.

Gracie Allen

I wanted to give birth as opposed to being delivered.

Ricki Lake

I'm not interested in being wonder woman in the delivery room. Give me drugs.

Madonna

Suddenly she was here. And I was no longer pregnant; I was a mother. I never believed in miracles before.

Ellen Greene

My mother groaned, my father wept, into the dangerous world I leapt; helpless, naked, piping loud, like a fiend hid in cloud.

William Blake

A male gynaecologist is like an auto mechanic who never owned a car.

Carrie Snow

Childbearing is glorified in part because women die from it.

Andrea Dworkin

These wretched babies don't come until they are ready.

Queen Elizabeth II

Good work Mary, we all knew you had it in you.

Dorothy Parker

Ladies are requested not to have children at the bar.

Sign in a Norwegian cocktail bar

Yes, hell exists. It is not a fairy tale. One indeed burns there. This hell is not at the end of life. It is here. At the beginning. Hell is what the infant must experience before he gets to us.

Dr Frederick Leboyer, French obstetrician

Giving birth was easier than having a tattoo.

Nicole Appleton

It is somehow reassuring to discover that the word 'travel' is derived from 'travail', denoting the pains of childbirth.

Jessica Mitford

Speech-making is exactly like childbirth. You are so glad to get it over with.

John Barrymore

The pains of childbirth were altogether different from the enveloping effects of other kinds of pain. These were pains one could follow with one's mind.

Margaret Mead

Death and taxes and childbirth? There's never any convenient time for any of them!

Margaret Mitchell

He doesn't speak, the newborn? Why his entire being shouts out, 'Don't touch me! Don't touch me!' And yet at the same time, imploringly, begging, 'Don't leave me! Don't leave me!' ... This is birth. This is the torture, the Calvary.

Dr Frederick Leboyer, French obstetrician

A woman when she is in travail hath sorrow, because her hour is come: but as soon as she is delivered of the child, she remembereth no more the anguish, for joy that a man is born into the world.

John 16:21

If men had to have babies they would only ever have one each.

Princess Diana

Although present on the occasion, I have no clear recollection of the events leading up to it.

Winston Churchill, discussing his own birth

The best way to avoid a Caesarean is to stay out of the hospital.

Brooke Sanders Purves

We have a secret in our culture, and it's not that birth is painful. It's that women are strong.

Laura Stavoe Harm

Just as a woman's heart knows how and when to pump, her lungs to inhale, and her hand to pull back from fire, so she knows when and how to give birth.

Virginia Di Orio

The same movements that get the baby in, get the baby out.

From Birthing Within

I think of birth as the search for a larger apartment.

Rita Mae Brown

Birth is violent, whether it be the birth of a child, or the birth of an idea.

Marianne Williamson

I was born at the age of 12 on the Metro-Goldwyn-Mayer lot.

Judy Garland

All birth is unwilling.

Pearl S. Buck

From beginning to end this is a blood-smeared voyage, this begetting and birthing and moving away.

Barbara Lazear Ascher

When I was giving birth the nurse asked, 'Still think blondes have more fun?'

Joan Rivers

If you lay down the baby will never come out.

Native American saying

There is power that comes to women when they give birth. They don't ask for it, it simply invades them. Accumulates like clouds on the horizon and passes through, carrying the child with it.

Sheryl Feldman

Childbirth classes neglect to teach one critical skill: how to breathe, count and swear all at the same time.

Linda Fiterman

Prepared childbirth is a contradiction in terms.

Joyce Armor

I'd be happy to stand next to any man I know in one of those labour rooms the size of a Volkswagen and whisper, 'No dear, you don't really need the Demerol; just relax and do your second stage breathing.'

Anna Quindlen

Our Lamaze instructor … assured our class … that our cervix muscles would become 'naturally numb' as they swelled and stretched, and deep breathing would turn the final explosions of pain into 'manageable discomfort'. This description turned out to be as accurate as, say a steward advising passengers aboard the *Titanic* to prepare for a brisk but bracing swim.

Mary Kay Blakely

I had a Jewish delivery: they knock you out with the first pain; they wake you up when the hairdresser shows.

Joan Rivers

Have you ever tried getting out of your car through the exhaust pipe?

Murphy Brown

If men had babies maternity leave would be in the Bill of Rights.

Corky Sherwood Forest

There's an African story of birth where the women gather and send you across the river, and as you walk across this log across the river you head out with these women. As you go across on the narrowest part you're alone. No one can be there with you, and as you emerge on to the other side of the river, all the women who have ever given birth are there to greet you.

Liz Koch

In my last stage of labour I threatened to take my husband to court for concealing a lethal weapon in his boxer shorts.

Linda Fiterman

As they started to clean it off … I went over to my wife, kissed her gently on the lips, and said, 'Darling, I love you very much. You just had a lizard.'

Bill Cosby

I already know how to breathe, and I'm the last person that needs to learn how to push.

Murphy Brown

Birthday parties are a lot like childbirth. After both events you solemnly swear you'll never make that mistake again.

Linda Fiterman

'Oh wow, three hours and still no baby. Ugh, the miracle of birth sure is a snooze fest.'

Phoebe, Friends

Having a baby is like trying to push a grand piano through a transom.

Alice Roosevelt Longworth

Giving birth is little more than a set of muscular contractions granting passage of a child. Then the mother is born.

Erma Bombeck

The old system of having a baby was much better than the new system, the old system being characterized by the fact that the man didn't have to watch.

Dave Barry

Ordering a man to write a poem is like commanding a pregnant woman to give birth to a red-headed child.

Carl Sandburg

Marshall, when you were born there was no such thing as stirrups in the delivery room; if there had been, I assure you, I would have slapped your bottom goodbye and rode right off into the sunset!

Mother B, Filthy Rich

Labour Intensive

I haven't been this shocked since well I gave birth to you: I thought you were wind, I very nearly called you Fart.

Linda, Gimme, Gimme, Gimme

I was born by Caesarean section, but you can't really tell … except that when I leave my house, I always go out the window.

Steven Wright

People are giving birth under water now. They say it's less traumatic for the baby because it's in water, then it comes out into water. I guess it would be less traumatic for the baby, but certainly more traumatic for the other people in the pool.

Elayne Boosler

My wife – God bless her – was in labour for thirty-two hours. And I was faithful to her the entire time.

Jonathan Katz

My sister was in labour for thirty-six hours. Ow! She got wheeled out of delivery, looked at me and said, 'Adopt.'

Caroline Rhea

If you don't yell during labour, you're a fool. I screamed. Oh, how I screamed. And that was just during the conception.

Joan Rivers

The idea with natural childbirth is to avoid drugs so the mother can share the first intimate moments after birth with the baby and the father and the obstetrician and the standby anaesthesiologist and the nurses and the person who cleans the floor.

Dave Barry

The Caesarean section is a district in Rome.

Exam paper answer

Open All Hours Breastfeeding

There are three reasons for breastfeeding: the milk is always at the right temperature; it comes in attractive containers; and the cat can't get it.

Irene Chalmers

There is no finer investment for any community than putting milk into babies.

Winston Churchill

My mother never breastfed me. She told me she liked me as a friend.

Rodney Dangerfield

Breastfeeding should not be attempted by fathers with hairy chests, since they can make the baby sneeze and give it wind.

Mike Harding

May earth provide us with all the things of our requirements just like a mother who breastfeeds her child.

Atharva Veda

My opinion is that anyone offended by breastfeeding is staring too hard.

Dave Allen

Lady Madonna, baby at your breast,
Wonders how you managed to feed the rest.

Paul McCartney

No one who has seen a baby sinking back satiated from the breast and falling asleep with flushed cheeks and a blissful smile can escape the reflection that this picture persists as a prototype of the expression of sexual satisfaction in later life.

Sigmund Freud

Never forget … breastfeeding is a confidence trick.

WHO handout

Pacifiers are sugarless gum for babies – an imitation of what a baby really needs. You already have two of the real things.

Diane Wiessinger

In short, breastfeeding occurs above the eyebrows as much or more than it occurs in the mammary glands.

Judithe A. Thompson

A babe at the breast is as much pleasure as the bearing is pain.

Marion Zimmer Bradley

Children suck the mother when they are young and the father when they are old.

English proverb

The babe at first feeds upon the mother's bosom, but is always on her heart.

Henry Ward Beecher

You cannot have power for good without having power for evil too. Even mother's milk nourishes murderers as well as heroes.

George Bernard Shaw

People need to understand that when they're deciding between breastmilk and formula, they're not deciding between Coke and Pepsi ... They're choosing between a live, pure substance and a dead substance made with the cheapest oils available.

Chele Marmet, lactation consultant

Anyone who has breastfed knows two things for sure: the baby wants to be fed at the most inopportune times, and in the most inopportune places, and the baby will prevail.

Anna Quindlen

There is no dream of love, however ideal it may be, which does not end up with a fat, greedy baby hanging from the breast.

Charles Baudelaire

And to think I breastfed you!

Mother B, Filthy Rich

In at the Deep End
Bringing Home Baby

Whenever I held my newborn baby in my arms, I used to think that what I said and did to him could have an influence not only on him but on all whom he met, not only for a day or a month or a year, but for all eternity – a very challenging and exciting thought for a mother.

Rose Kennedy

I stand on the sidewalk watching it because the responsibility is mine and I must, I take a very firm hold on the handles of the baby carriage and I wheel it into the traffic.

Grace Abbott

You can sort of be married, you can sort of be divorced, you can sort of be living together, but you can't sort of have a baby.

David Shire

A Harvard Medical School study has determined that rectal thermometers are still the best way to tell a baby's temperature. Plus, it really teaches the baby who's boss.

Tina Fey

I can't think why mothers love them. All babies do is leak at both ends.

Douglas Feaver

I don't know why they say, 'You have a baby.' The baby has you.

Anon.

I visited those friends who'd just had a baby, and she was washing dishes and he was cleaning the house, and I burst with happiness. And in their minds, they were in this terrible domestic rut.

Josh Lucas

Insomnia: a contagious disease often transmitted from babies to parents.

Shannon Fife

I remember leaving the hospital thinking, 'Wait, are they just going to let me walk off with him? I don't know beans about babies. I don't have a licence to do this.'

Anne Tyler

The worst feature of a new baby is its mother singing.

Kin Hubbard

The hot, moist smell of babies fresh from naps.

Barbara Lazear Ascher

I understood once I held a baby in my arms, why some people have the need to keep having them.

Spalding Gray

I got introduced to audiobooks because of having a baby.

Susie Bright

Who is getting more pleasure from this rocking, the baby or me?

Nancy Thayer

It is true that you may occasionally overhear a mother say, 'Children must have their naps, it is mother who knows best.' When what she really means is that she needs a rest.

Anon.

I think at a child's birth, if a mother could ask a fairy godmother to endow it with the most useful gift, that gift would be curiosity.

Eleanor Roosevelt

In the sheltered simplicity of the first days after a baby is born, one sees again the magical closed circle, the miraculous sense of two people existing only for each other.

Anne Morrow Lindbergh

I feel whole at last.

Meg Matthews

It sometimes happens, even in the best of families, that a baby is born. This is not necessarily cause for alarm. The important thing is to keep your wits about you and borrow some money.

Elinor Goulding Smith

Holding your firstborn, your wife looks at you through different eyes, a traveller from another country. The mothering cues are clearly rooted very deep in the female psyche.

Charlton Heston

Claudia ... remembered that when she'd had her first baby she had realized with astonishment that the perfect couple consisted of a mother and child and not, as she had always supposed, a man and woman.

Alice Thomas Ellis

My mother says I didn't open my eyes for eight days after I was born, but when I did, the first thing I saw was an engagement ring. I was hooked.

Elizabeth Taylor

When you have a baby, you set off an explosion in your marriage, and when the dust settles, your marriage is different from what it was. Not better, necessarily; but different.

Nora Ephron

What is the use of a newborn child?

Benjamin Franklin

In a big family the first child is kind of like the first pancake. If it's not perfect, there are a lot more coming along.

Antonin Scalia

Our planning may leave something to be desired, but our designs, thank God, have been flawless.

Noor, Queen of Jordan, having given birth to her fourth child in six years

Athens holds sway over all Greece; I dominate Athens; my wife dominates me; our newborn son dominates her.

Themistocles, explaining why his newborn son ruled all Greece

There is nothing like a newborn baby to renew your spirit – and to buttress your resolve to make the world a better place.

Virginia Kelley

The absolute dependence of a newborn infant inspired many things in me, but it did not activate any magical knowledge about what to do for the next twenty years.

Mary Kay Blakely

A healthy newborn has been delivered in a more or less satisfying fashion. The baby is feeding well, has short nails and a clean bottom, and has not drowned. Now what?

Sandra Scarr

Parents sometimes think of newborns as helpless creatures, but in fact parents' behaviour is much more under the infant's control than the reverse. Does he come running when you cry?

Sandra Scarr

I have always felt that too much time was given before the birth, which is spent in learning things like how to breathe in and out with your husband (I had my baby when they gave you a shot in the hip and you didn't wake up until the kid was at school), and not enough time given to how to mother after the baby is born.

Erma Bombeck

Babies are beautiful, wonderful, exciting, enchanting, extraordinary little creatures – who grow up into ordinary folk like us.

Doris Dyson

Most of us would do more for our babies than we have ever been willing to do for anyone, even ourselves.

Polly Berrien Berends

Someone once told me that children are like heroin. You always want more. Yet firstborns are special because you'll never have your first child again.

Sarah Jessica Parker

A baby's a full-time job for three adults. Nobody tells you that when you're pregnant, or you'd probably jump off a bridge.

Erica Jong

Child rearing myth number one: Labour ends when the baby is born.

Anon.

When mother boasts cheerfully, 'Johnny is just crazy about his new little sister ... You love her, don't you, dear?' Johnny hasn't much choice but to lie like a gentleman.

Leontine Young

The conscientious mother of this age approaches the birth of her first baby with two ideas firmly in mind. One is that she will raise the baby by schedule. The other, that she will not let it suck its thumb.

Gladys D. Schultz

I was just learning to take care of the belly-button stump, when it fell off. I had just learned to make formula really efficiently, when Sarah stopped using it.

Anne C. Weisberg and Carol A. Buckler

If you desire to drain to the dregs the fullest cup of scorn and hatred that a fellow human being can pour out for you, let a young mother hear you call dear baby 'it'.

Jerome K. Jerome

I could still remember how having a two-day-old baby makes you feel faintly sorry for everyone else, stuck in their wan unmiraculous lives.

Marni Jackson

Sister Peters says that newborn babies mostly sleep well. It is only when they get home they start bawling their heads off.

Elizabeth Jolly

After you have a baby, in a few months you work your way up to getting dressed. Then, after a few more months, you can start doing your hair, maybe putting on makeup a few times. But you never, ever get back to accessorizing.

Michelle Pfeiffer

She made me a security blanket when I was born. That faded green blanket lasted just long enough for me to realize that the security part came from her.

Alexander Crane

Meconium happens.

Anon.

The joy of having a baby today can only be expressed in two words: tax deduction.

Anon.

You know that having a baby has drastically changed your life when you and your husband go on a date to Wal-Mart on double coupon day.

Linda Fiterman

A baby will make love stronger, days shorter, nights longer, bankroll smaller, home happier, clothes shabbier, the past forgotten, and the future worth living for.

Anon.

A soiled baby, with a neglected nose, cannot be conscientiously regarded as a thing of beauty.

Mark Twain, replying to a young mother

There are lots of things that you can brush under the carpet about yourself until you're faced with somebody whose needs won't be put off.

Angela Carter, on being a mother for the first time, at age 43

The first time many women hold their tiny babies, they are apt to feel as clumsy and incompetent as any man. The difference is that our culture tells them they're not supposed to feel that way.

Pamela Patrick Novotny

You may be used to a day that includes answering eleven phone calls, attending two meetings, and writing three reports; when you are at home with an infant you will feel you have accomplished quite a lot if you have a shower and a sit-down meal in the same day.

Anne C. Weisberg

A baby is a blank cheque made payable to the human race.

Barbara Christine Seifert

We learn from experience. You never wake up a second baby just to see it smile.

Anon.

What good mothers … instinctively feel like doing for their babies is usually best after all.

Benjamin Spock

The naïve notion that a mother naturally acquires the complex skills of childrearing simply because she has given birth now seems as absurd to me as enrolling in a nine-month class in composition and imagining that at the end of the course you are now prepared to begin writing *War and Peace*.

Mary Kay Blakely

Post-natal Degeneration

When a woman is twenty, a child deforms her, when she is thirty, he preserves her, and when forty, he makes her young again.

Leon Blum

It's a huge change for your body. You don't even want to look in the mirror after you've had a baby, because your stomach is just hanging there like a Shar-Pei.

Cindy Crawford

The breasts go first, and then the waist and then the butt. Nobody ever tells you that you get a butt when you get pregnant.

Elle Macpherson

CHARLOTTE: What kind of diet book are you looking for?
MIRANDA: I don't know. Something with a title like 'How to Lose That Baby Fat by Sitting on Your Ass'.

Sex in the City

People said I'd slim down quickly. Nobody told me it was because I'd never have time to eat.

Anon.

You've been a fantastic mother. You've let them ruin your figure. Your stomach is stretched beyond recognition, you've got tits down to your knees and what for, for God's sake?

Patsy to Edina, Absolutely Fabulous

Wishful Thinking
Sex After Childbirth

It's so long since I've had sex, I've forgotten who ties up who.

Joan Rivers

It's sad that children cannot know their parents when they were younger; when they were loving, courting, and being nice to one another. By the time children are old enough to observe, the romance has all too often faded or gone underground.

Virginia Satir

No woman needs intercourse; few women escape it.

Andrea Dworkin

Of course I don't always enjoy being a mother. At those times my husband and I hole up somewhere in the wine country, eat, drink, make mad love and pretend we were born sterile and raise poodles.

Dorothy DeBolt, on receiving 1980 National Mother's Day Committee Award as the natural mum of six and adoptive mum of fourteen

Vibrators. I think they are great. They keep you out of stupid sex. I'd pitch them to anyone.

Anne Heche

Older women are best, because they always think they may be doing it for the last time.

Ian Fleming

Before we make love my husband takes a painkiller.

Joan Rivers

My sons think it's a fireman's pole but I forgot to cut a hole through the ground into the kitchen.

Pamela Anderson

Birth Control

My best birth control now is just to leave the lights on.

Joan Rivers

The best contraception for old people is nudity.

Phyllis Diller

The best contraceptive is the word no – repeated frequently.

Margaret Smith

A woman who took the pill with a glass of pond water has been diagnosed three months stagnant.

The Two Ronnies

The most effective form of birth control I know is spending the day with my kids.

Jill Bensley

Contraceptives should be used on every conceivable occasion.

Spike Milligan

We want far better reasons for having children than not knowing how to prevent them.

Dora Winifred Black Russell

Have you noticed that all the people in favour of birth control are already born?

Benny Hill

It is now quite lawful for a Catholic woman to avoid pregnancy by a resort to mathematics, though she is still forbidden to resort to physics and chemistry.

Henry Louis Mencken

Birth control that really works: every night before we go to bed we spend an hour with our kids.

Roseanne Barr

No woman can call herself free who does not own and control her own body. No woman can call herself free until she can choose consciously whether she will or will not be a mother.

Margaret Sanger

I rely on my personality for birth control.

Liz Winston

Would you be more careful if it was you that got pregnant?

British Family Planning Association, urging men to use birth control

When modern woman discovered the orgasm it was (combined with modern birth control) perhaps the biggest single nail in the coffin of male dominance.

Eva Figes

Children troop down from heaven because God wills it.

Archbishop Patrick Hayes, battling with birth-control pioneers in the 1920s

I don't think Christians should use birth control. You consummate your marriage as often as you like and if you have babies, you have babies.

Anon.

When my mom found my diaphragm, I told her it was a bathing cap for my cat.

Liz Winston

Given a choice between hearing my daughter say 'I'm pregnant' or 'I used a condom', most mothers would get up in the middle of the night and buy them themselves.

Joycelyn Elders

The surest form of birth control is often a good argument.

Anon.

The best form of contraception is a pill – held firmly between the knees.

Anon.

I'm glad I'm a woman because I don't have to worry about getting men pregnant.

Nell Dunn

[I advise keeping] four feet on the floor and all hands on deck.

Ann Landers

I sometimes think that being widowed is God's way of telling you to come off the pill.

Victoria Wood

Driving You Potty

Laughter is like changing a baby's diaper. It doesn't permanently solve any problems, but it makes things more acceptable for a while.

Anon.

One year, I'd completely lost my bearings trying to follow potty training instruction from a psychiatric expert. I was stuck on step one, which stated without an atom of irony: 'Before you begin, remove all stubbornness from the child.'

Mary Kay Blakely

The area [of toilet training] is one where a child really does possess the power to defy … And the child has most of the ammunition!

Dorothy Corkville Briggs

I was toilet trained at gunpoint.

Billy Braver

Like many other women, I could not understand why every man who changed a diaper has felt compelled to write a book about it.

Barbara Ehrenreich

To be perfectly, brutally honest, those of us who are still carrying diapers everywhere we go are not at our most scintillating time of life …

Louise Lague

I didn't want to be so short-sighted as to be worrying about diaper rash, and not taking care of bigger things like nuclear war.

Barbara Donachy

Changing a diaper is a lot like getting a present from your grandmother – you're not sure what you've got but you're pretty sure you're not going to like it.

Jeff Foxworthy

No one likes change but babies in diapers.

Barbara Johnson

One of the most important things to remember about infant care is to not change nappies in midstream.

Anon.

Most men cannot change a diaper without subsequently renting an airplane that trails a banner that says 'I CHANGED A DIAPER.'

Anna Quindlen

Diaper backward spells repaid. Think about it.

Marshall Mcluhan

A bit of talcum
Is always walcum.

Ogden Nash

We used chamber pots a good deal ... My mother ... loved to repeat: 'When did the queen reign over China?' This whimsical and harmless scatological pun was my first introduction to the wonderful world of verbal transformations.

Angela Carter

Kids: Who'd Have 'Em?

Children seldom misquote you. They more often repeat word for word what you shouldn't have said.

Mae Maloo

Do not, on a rainy day, ask your child what he feels like doing, because I assure you that what he feels like doing, you won't feel like watching.

Fran Lebowitz

There is no reciprocity. Men love women, women love children. Children love hamsters.

Alice Thomas Ellis

Don't tell your 2-year-old she's driving you nuts. She just might say, 'Mama nuts' to everyone she meets.

Jan Blaustone

Children are a life sentence.

Marilyn Hahn

Girls are difficult to raise. Boys are easier. True, boys can be rambunctious, but they're simple and they don't have periods.

Linda Knight

My kids always perceived the bathroom as a place where you wait it out until all the groceries are unloaded from the car.

Erma Bombeck

My kids are the reason for everything. The reason everything is out of place, broken and dirty.

Anon.

The mother, poor invaded soul, finds even the bathroom door no bar to hammering little hands.

Charlotte Perkins Gilman

Children ask better questions than adults. 'May I have a cookie?' 'Why is the sky blue?' and 'What does a cow say?' are far more likely to elicit a cheerful response than 'Where is your manuscript?' 'Why haven't you called?' and 'Who's your lawyer?'

Fran Lebowitz

See the mind of a 5-year-old as a volcano with two vents: destructiveness and creativeness.

Sylvia Aston Warner

Being a child is horrible. It is slightly better than being a tree or a piece of heavy machinery but not half as good as being a domestic cat.

Julie Burchill

I've seen kids ride bicycles, run, play ball, set up a camp, swing, fight a war, swim and race for eight hours … yet have to be driven to the garbage can.

Erma Bombeck

Children are not things to be moulded, but are people to be unfolded.

Jess Lair

Children are like sponges; they absorb all your strength and leave you limp … But give them a squeeze and you get it all back.

Ann Van Tassells

Toddlers have to learn and endlessly review – why you can't put bottles with certain labels in your mouth, why you have to sit on the potty, why you can't take whatever you want in the store, why you don't hit your friends – by the time we got to why you can't drop your peas, well, I was dropping a few myself.

Mary Kay Blakely

Toddlers are more likely to eat healthy food if they find it on the floor.

Jan Blaustone

Youngsters of the age of 2 or 3 are endowed with extraordinary strength. They can lift a dog twice their own weight and dump him into the bathtub.

Erma Bombeck

A child is someone who stands halfway between an adult and a TV set.

Anon.

Perhaps parents would enjoy their children more if they stopped to realize that the film of childhood can never be run through for a second showing.

Evelyn Nown

Whether your child is 3 or 13, don't rush in to rescue him until you know he's done all he can to rescue himself.

Barbara F. Meltz

Never allow your child to call you by your first name. He hasn't known you long enough.

Fran Lebowitz

It puzzles me how a child can see a dairy bar three miles away, but cannot see a 4 by 6 rug that has scrunched up under his feet and has been dragged through two rooms.

Erma Bombeck

Notoriously insensitive to subtle shifts in mood, children will persist in discussing the colour of a recently sighted cement mixer long after one's own interest in the topic has waned.

Fran Lebowitz

Children always understand. They have open minds. They have built-in shit detectors.

Madonna

Children see everything according to how it impinges on them.

Nigella Lawson

No animal is so inexhaustible as an excited infant.

Amy Leslie

Anyone who thinks the art of conversation is dead ought to tell a child to go to bed.

Anon.

I love this child. Red-haired – patient and gentle like her mother – fey and funny like her father. When she giggles I can hear him when he and I were young. I am part of this child. It may be only because we share genes and that therefore smell familiar to each other … But for now, it's jelly beans and 'Old MacDonald' that unite us.

Robert Fulghum

Kids can be a pain in the neck when they're not a lump in your throat.

Barbara Johnson

The fundamental job of a toddler is to rule the universe.

Anon.

Even when freshly washed and relieved of all obvious confections, children tend to be sticky.

Fran Lebowitz

Maternal Moments

People always talked about a mother's uncanny ability to read her children, but that was nothing compared to how children could read their mothers.

Anne Tyler

There is only one pretty child in the world, and every mother has it.

Chinese proverb

That's one thing I find about having children – it does unlock a door that separates you from other women who've had children.

Rebecca Miller

What a difference it makes to come home to a child

Margaret Fuller

Life is a corrupting process from the time a child learns to play his mother off against his father in the politics of when to go to bed; he who fears corruption fears life.

Saul David Alinsky

Who takes the child by the hand takes the mother by the heart.

German proverb

We've begun to raise daughters more like sons ... but few have the courage to raise our sons more like our daughters.

Gloria Steinem

Until her child goes to school, the Japanese mother devotes herself to the rearing of the child ... Then she says, 'After all I've done for you, don't disappoint me.' She's like the Jewish mother who says, 'What do you mean you're not hungry – after I've slaved all day over a hot stove for you.'

Jerome Kagan

'Never hug and kiss your children! Mother love may make your children's infancy unhappy and prevent them from pursuing a career or getting married!' That's total hogwash, of course. But it shows an extreme example of what state-of-the-art 'scientific' parenting was supposed to be in early twentieth-century America.

Lawrence Kutner

As Anna Freud remarked, the toddler who wanders off into some other aisle, feels lost, and screams anxiously for his mother never says 'I got lost,' but accusingly says 'You lost me!'

Bruno Bettelheim

What did that mean, to kiss? You put your face up like that to say goodnight and then his mother put her face down. That was to kiss. His mother put her lips on his cheek; her lips were soft and they wetted his cheek; and they made a tiny little noise: kiss. Why did people do that with their two faces?

James Joyce

Before I became a mother I was such a free spirit. I used to say, 'No man will ever dominate me.' Now I have a 6-year-old master.

Sally Diaz

The illusions of childhood are necessary experiences; a child should not be denied a balloon because an adult knows that sooner or later it will burst.

Marcelene Cox

Parents of young children should realize that few people, and maybe no one, will find their children as enchanting as they do.

Barbara Walters

Likely as not, the child you can do least with will do the most to make you proud.

Mignon McLaughlin

I always wanted children, but not until they were actually part of my life did I realize that I could love that fiercely, or get that angry.

Cokie Roberts

To nourish children and raise them against odds is in any time, any place, more valuable than to fix bolts in cars or design nuclear weapons.

Marilyn French

We worry about what a child will be tomorrow, yet we forget he is someone today.

Stacia Tauscher

The rules for parents are three … love, limit, and let them be.

Elaine M. Ward

Children are the sum of what mothers contribute to their lives.

Anon.

Whoever Said …

… it takes about six weeks to get back to normal after you've had a baby … doesn't know that once you're a mother, normal is history.

... you learn to be a mother by instinct ... never took a 3-year-old shopping.

... being a mother is boring ... never rode in a car driven by a teenager with a driver's licence.

... if you're a good mother, your child will turn out good ... must think a child comes with directions and a guarantee.

... 'Good mothers never raise their voices' ... never came out the back door just in time to see her child hit a golf ball through the neighbour's window.

... you don't need an education to be a mother ... has never helped a fourth grader with his maths homework.

... you can't love a fifth child as much as you love the first ... doesn't have five children.

... the hardest part of being a mother is labour and delivery ... has never watched her baby walk through the school gates for the first time.

... a mother can stop worrying after her child gets married ... doesn't know that marriage adds a new son- or daughter-in-law to a mother's heartstrings.

... a mother's job is done when her last child leaves home ... doesn't have grandchildren.

... your mother knows you love her, so you don't need to tell her ... isn't a mother.

All anon.

The Wonder Years

Mom, I'll always love you, but I'll never forgive you for cleaning my face with spit on a hanky.

Anon.

When I was a girl I only had two friends, and they were imaginary. And they would only play with each other.

Rita Rudner

My mother's obsession with the good scissors always scared me a bit. It implied that somewhere in the house there lurked: the evil scissors.

Tony Martin

Little girl's definition of conscience: something that makes you tell your mother before your brother or sister does.

Anon.

When you've seen a nude infant doing a backward somersault you know why clothing exists.

Stephen Fry

A sweater is a garment worn by a child when the mother feels chilly.

Barbara Johnson

Boys are found everywhere – on top of, underneath, inside of, climbing on, swinging from, running around or jumping to. Mothers love them, little girls hate them, older sisters and brothers tolerate them, adults ignore them and Heaven protects them.

Alan Marshall Beck

Childhood smells of perfume and brownies.

David Leavitt

Things You Should Never Say to a Mother

I wouldn't let my child speak to me like that.

Is one of your twins smarter than the other?

Why don't you dress your twins the same?

Is your baby supposed to be that fat?

She doesn't look like you – is she adopted?

Are you pregnant again?

Do you know who the real mum is?

You've got your hands full.

Skool Rools

Parents learn a lot from their children about coping with life.

Muriel Spark

If there were no schools to take the children away from home part of the time, the insane asylum would be filled with mothers.

Edgar Watson Howe

The mother's heart is the child's schoolroom.

Henry Ward Beecher

That best academy, a mother's knee.

James Russell Lowell

Children learn to smile from their parents.

Shinichi Suzuki

You may have tangible wealth untold; caskets of jewels and coffers of gold. Richer than I you can never be, I had a mother who read to me.

Strickland Gillian

Never help a child with a task at which he feels he can succeed.

Maria Montessori

I never went to school beyond the third grade, but my mother taught me the difference between right and wrong.

Joe Lewis

If I do my homework on the bus, my mum never believes me.

Adam, age 9

The easiest way for your children to learn about money is for you not to have any.

Katharine Whitehorn

A mother is a person who if she is not there when you get home from school you wouldn't know how to get your dinner, and you wouldn't feel like eating it anyway.

Anon.

I hated school. Even to this day, when I see a school bus it's just depressing to me. The poor little kids.

Dolly Parton

Mums are not so much concerned about education, paediatrics, child poverty, law and order and the arms race as about Emily and Robert and Imram and Njoroge. Which is, after all, the same thing.

Clare D'Arcy

Never tell your kids how well you did at school. Mum still has your reports.

Itoko Fujita

My mother never gave up on me. I messed up in school so much they were sending me home, but my mother sent me right back.

Denzel Washington

It's a mistake to think that once you're done with school you need never learn anything new.

Sophia Loren

Mothers' Wit

There is no influence so powerful as that of the mother, but next in rank of efficacy is that of schoolmaster.

Sarah Josepha Hale

A little boy came home and told his mother he had gotten first prize in an examination. The question had been 'How many legs does a horse have?' He had answered, 'Three.' When his mother asked how he had gotten the first prize, he replied that all the other children had said, 'Two.'

Richard Kehl

I always tell people that I became a writer not because I went to school but because my mother took me to the library.

Sandra Cisneros

The kids were very young and I didn't want to be one of those mums who turn up at the schoolyard covered in tattoos.

Sharon Osbourne

My mother … believed fiction gave one an unrealistic view of the world. Once she caught me reading a novel and chastised me: 'Never let me catch you doing that again, remember what happened to Emma Bovary.'

Angela Carter

MAX DETWEILER: I get a fiendish delight thinking of you as the mother of seven. How do you plan to do it?
THE BARONESS: Darling, haven't you heard of a delightful little thing called boarding school?

The Sound of Music

'Don't teach my boy poetry,' an English mother recently wrote the Provost of Harrow. 'Don't teach my boy poetry; he is going to stand for Parliament.' Well, perhaps she was right – but if more politicians knew poetry, and more poets knew politics, I am convinced the world would be a little better place to live.

Senator John F. Kennedy

My mother made me a scientist without ever intending to. Every other Jewish mother in Brooklyn would ask her child after school: 'So? Did you learn anything today?' But not my mother. 'Izzy,' she would say, 'did you ask a good question today?'

Isidor Isaac Rabi

A mother once asked a clergyman when she should begin the education of her child, who, she told him was 4 years old. 'Madam,' was the reply, 'you have lost three years already. From the first smile that gleams over an infant's cheek, your opportunity begins.'

Archbishop Richard Whately

Children used to be let out of school so they could work – now they are sent there so their mother can.

Anon.

We are now at a point where we must educate our children in what no one knew yesterday, and prepare our schools for what no one knows yet.

Margaret Mead

I suppose it is because nearly all children go to school nowadays, and have things arranged for them, that they seem so forlornly unable to produce their own ideas.

Agatha Christie

If you are truly serious about preparing your child for the future, don't teach him to subtract – teach him to deduct.

Fran Lebowitz

Everyone is in awe of the lion tamer in a cage with half a dozen lions – everyone but a school bus driver.

Anon.

TEACHER: Come and join in, sweetheart.
3-YEAR-OLD AT NURSERY: No thanks, I don't like you or your nursery.

Anon.

... as for helping me in the outside world, the Convent taught me only that if you spit on a pencil eraser, it will erase ink.

Dorothy Parker

The reason you want your kids to pay attention in school is you haven't the faintest idea how to do their homework.

Hazel Scott

If you must give your child lessons, send him to driving school. He is far more likely to end up owning a Datsun than he is a Stradivarius.

Fran Lebowitz

I spend a lot of time at my son's school and I really wanted to do a movie that the kids could see. The good thing about being my age and not having to be the ingénue any more is that I get to be a mom. I get to have kids in my movies.

Virginia Masden

Rarely is the question asked: is our children learning?

George W. Bush

I was coming home from kindergarten – well mom told me it was kindergarten. I found out later I had been working in a factory for ten years. It's good for a kid to know how to make gloves.

Ellen DeGeneres

A mother is neither cocky, nor proud, because she knows the school principal may call at any minute to report that her child had just driven a motorcycle through the gymnasium.

Mary Kay Blakely

Mothers' Classics and Clichés

Someday your face will freeze like that!

What if everyone jumped off a cliff ... Would you do it, too?

You're going to put your eye out with that thing!

Don't put that in your mouth ... you don't know where it's been.

Mothers' Wit

Did you flush?

I hope someday you have children just like you.

If I have to get out of this chair!

Come over by there to over by yur; we don't want to take you home losted now, do we?

Overheard on Barry Island beach, South Wales

Don't eat that, you'll get worms!

A little soap and water never killed anyone!

You could have been dead in a ditch for all I knew!

Don't use that tone with me!

You won't be happy until you break that, will you!

You'd lose your head if it wasn't attached to your shoulders!

You'd better wipe that smile off your face before I come and do it for you!

What part of the word *no* don't you understand?

Why? Because I said so, that's why!

Now come back downstairs and go back up again *without* stamping your feet!

I've told you a million times, don't exaggerate!

Go tidy your room – and be ruthless with it!

Your eyes are bigger than your belly!

It'll end in tears!

The Other Mother

Only Adam had no mother-in-law. That's how we know he lived in paradise.

Old Yiddish saying

I told my mother-in-law that my house was her house, and she said, 'Get the hell off my property.'

Joan Rivers

We never make sport of religion, politics, race or mothers. A mother never gets hit with a custard pie. Mothers-in-law – yes. But mothers – never.

Anon.

Conscience is a mother-in-law whose visit never ends.

Henry Louis Mencken

There is but one good mother-in-law and she is dead.

English proverb

Mother-in law: a woman who destroys her son-in-law's peace of mind by giving him a piece of hers.

Anon.

The mother-in law frequently forgets that she was a daughter-in-law.

Anon.

English law prohibits a man from marrying his mother-in-law. This is our idea of useless legislation.

Anon.

Never rely on the glory of the morning or the smiles of your mother-in-law.

Japanese proverb

Of all the peoples whom I have studied, from city dwellers to cliff dwellers, I always find that at least 50 per cent would prefer to have at least one jungle between themselves and their mother-in-law.

Margaret Mead

Having a baby changes the way you view your in-laws. I love it when they come to visit now. They can hold the baby and I can go out.

Matthew Broderick

I just thought of something funny … your mother.

Cheech Marin

Be kind to your mother-in-law, but pay for her board at some good hotel.

Josh Billings

What a marvellous place to drop one's mother-in-law!

Marshal Foch, remarking on the Grand Canyon

But there, everything has its drawbacks, as the man said when his mother-in-law died, and they came down upon him for the funeral expenses.

Jerome K. Jerome

Back of every achievement is a proud wife and a surprised mother-in-law.

Brooks Hays

A person often catches a cold when a mother-in-law comes to visit. Patients mentioned mother-in-laws so often that we came to consider them a common cause of disease in the United States.

Thomas Holmes

I know a mother-in-law who sleeps with her glasses on, the better to see her son-in-law suffer in her dreams.

Ernest Coquelin

Happiness is seeing your mother-in-law's picture on the back of a milk carton.

Anon.

The awe and dread with which the untutored savage contemplates his mother-in-law are amongst the most familiar facts of anthropology.

Sir James George Frazer

To have one's mother-in-law in the country when one lives in Paris, and vice versa, is one of those strokes of luck that one encounters only too rarely.

Honoré de Balzac

Honolulu, it's got everything. Sand for the children, sun for the wife, sharks for the wife's mother.

Ken Dodd

Mothers' Wit

A mother-in-law and a daughter-in-law in one house are like two cats in a bag.

Yiddish proverb

A husband's mother and his wife had generally better be visitors than inmates.

Samuel Richardson

The wife's mother is always more prejudiced against the husband than even the most ill-treated wife. If I had my way, I am afraid I would abolish mothers-in-law entirely.

Geoffrey Wrangham

Unless one pretends to be stupid and deaf, it is difficult to be a mother-in-law or father-in-law.

Chinese proverb

Like the man who threw a stone at a bitch, but hit his step-mother, on which he exclaimed, 'Not so bad!'

Plutarch

My mother-in-law broke up my marriage. My wife came home from work one day and found me in bed with her.

Lenny Bruce

The chain of wedlock is so heavy that it takes two to carry it – and sometimes three.

Alexandre Dumas

Just because you are unemployed doesn't mean you are not doing anything useful. You are, for example, at least keeping your mother-in-law's wit sharp.

Marilyn Vos Savant

The Other Mother

My wife is the kind of girl who will not go anywhere without her mother, and her mother will go anywhere.

John Barrymore

As long as I was a daughter-in-law I never had a good mother-in-law, and as long as I was a mother-in-law I never had a good daughter-in-law.

Spanish proverb

Her mother keeps threatening to kill herself if she moves out; I think she should risk it.

Gary, Men Behaving Badly

I just saw all the animals in the neighbourhood running in circles, so I guess that means your mother will be arriving soon.

Dan, Roseanne

My mother-in-law works at Heathrow airport – sniffing luggage.

Anon.

Milwaukee, that's the town they built around your mother isn't it, Peg?

Al Bundy

Have I got a mother-in-law? She's so neat she puts paper under the cuckoo clock.

Henry Youngman

Mummy, Where Did I Come From?

Kids used to ask where they came from, now they tell you where to go.

Anon.

Don't bother discussing sex with small children. They rarely have anything to add.

Fran Lebowitz

I didn't know how babies were made until I was pregnant with my fourth child.

Loretta Lynn

Sex – the great inequality, the great miscalculator, the great irritator.

Enid Bagnold

I blame my mother for my poor sex life. All she told me was 'the man goes on top and the woman underneath'. For three years my husband and I slept in bunk beds.

Joan Rivers

If sex is such a natural phenomenon, how come there are so many books on how to do it?

Bette Midler

Literature is mostly about having sex and not much about having children. Life is the other way round.

David Lodge

EDINA: I did tell you the facts of life didn't I sweetie?
SAFFY: If you mean that time you sat on my bed and shook me awake at two in the morning, stoned out of your brain, and slurred into my ear, 'By the way sweetie, people have it off,' then yes, you told me the facts of life.

Absolutely Fabulous

My mom always taught me to be sweet and polite and cross my legs because it's what the guys like. Actually they like a raunchy girl once in a while.

Tiffani Amber Thiessen

It's very healthy for a young girl to be deterred from promiscuity by fear of contracting a painful, incurable disease ... even ten years later when she may be happily married.

Phyllis Schafly

Sexual enlightenment is justified in so far as girls cannot learn too soon how children come into the world.

Anon.

LITTLE GIRL: ... and then mummy kissed daddy, and the angel told the stork, and the stork flew down from heaven, and put the diamond in the cabbage patch, and the diamond turned into a baby.
PUGSLEY: Our parents are having a baby too.
WEDNESDAY: They had sex.

Addams Family Values

'Do you know who made you?' 'Nobody as I knows on,' said the child, with a short laugh. The idea appeared to amuse her considerably; for her eyes twinkled, and she added, 'I 'spect I growed. Don't think nobody never made me.'

Harriet Beecher Stowe

There's a time when you have to explain to your children why they're born, and it's a marvellous thing if you know the reason by then.

Hazel Scott

Hormone Hell

As a teenager you are at the last stage in your life when you will be happy to hear that the phone is for you.

Fran Lebowitz

Children aren't happy with nothing to ignore,
And that's what parents were created for.

Ogden Nash

Teenage boys, goaded by their surging hormones, run in packs like the primal horde. They have only a brief season of exhilarating liberty between control by their mothers and control by their wives.

Camille Paglia

You know your children are growing up when they stop asking you where they came from and refuse to tell you where they're going.

P.J. O'Rourke

By the time your kids are fit to live with, they live with somebody else.

K. Prieskorn

Parents are the bones on which children sharpen their teeth.

Peter Ustinov

The typical American boy would love to go to the moon, but hates to go to the supermarket for his mother.

Anon.

Small children give you headache; big children heartache.

Russian proverb

The invention of the teenager was a mistake. Once you identify a period of life in which people get to stay out late but don't have to pay taxes – naturally no one wants to live any other way.

Judith Martin

It is better to be black than gay, because when you're black you don't have to tell your mother.

Charles Pierce

It's difficult to decide whether growing pains are something teenagers have – or are.

Anon.

A child develops individuality long before he develops taste. I have seen my kid straggle into the kitchen in the morning with outfits that need only one accessory: an empty gin bottle.

Erma Bombeck

At 14 you don't need sickness or death for tragedy.

Jessamyn West

If you have never been hated by your child you have never been a parent.

Bette Davis

Adolescence is perhaps nature's way of preparing parents to welcome the empty nest.

Karen Savage and Patricia Adams

The troubles of adolescence eventually all go away – it's just like a really long, bad cold.

Dawn Ruelas

Small children disturb your sleep, big children your life.

Yiddish proverb

My adolescence progressed normally: enough misery to keep the death wish my usual state, an occasional high to keep me from actually taking the gas pipe.

Faye Moskowitz

Never lend your car to anyone to whom you have given birth.

Erma Bombeck

Raising teenagers is like nailing Jell-o to a tree.

Anon.

Mothers of teenagers know why animals eat their young.

Anon.

You have to hang on in there, because two or three years later, the gremlins will return your child, and he will be wonderful again.

Jill Eikenberry

Adolescence is just one big walking pimple.

Carole Burnett

An unsupervised teenager with a modem is as dangerous as an unsupervised teenager with a gun.

Gail Thackeray

At the moment that a boy of 13 is turning toward girls, a girl of 13 is turning on her mother. This girl can get rather unreasonable, often saying such comical things as 'Listen, this is my life!'

Bill Cosby

Spooky things happen in houses densely occupied by adolescent boys. When I checked out a four-inch dent in the living room ceiling one afternoon, even the kid still holding the baseball bat looked genuinely baffled about how he could possibly have done it.

Mary Kay Blakely

Adolescence is a period of rapid changes. Between the ages of 12 and 17, for example, it can age a mother by as much as twenty years.

Anon.

If you want to recapture your youth, just cut off his allowance.

Al Bernstein

Life was a lot simpler when what we honoured was father and mother rather than all major credit cards.

Robert Orben

Telling a teenager the facts of life is like giving a fish a bath.

Anon.

I became the Incredible Shrinking Mother the year they started junior high. If our relationship today depended on physical clout, I would have about the same influence with them that the republic of Liechtenstein has on world politics.

Mary Kay Blakely

One mother … was taken aback when she called, as her daughter was going out the door, 'Have a good time,' and her daughter angrily replied, 'Stop telling me what to do!'

Nancy Samalin

It isn't what a teenager knows that worries his parents. It's how he found out.

Ann Landers

It's always been my feeling that God lends you your children until they are about 18 years old. If you haven't made your point with them by then, it's too late.

Betty Ford

[One mother said her teenager] actually believes that he won't break out into acne because he is philosophically opposed to pimples.

Laurence Steinberg

For parents, the terrible twos are a psychological preview of puberty ... At the age of 2 or 3, children eat only bananas and refuse to get a haircut. Ten years later, they eat only bananas and refuse to get a haircut.

Carin Rubenstein

I had let pre-adolescence creep up on me without paying much attention – and I seriously underestimated this insidious phase of child development.

Susan Ferraro

Warnings about the 'wrong crowd' ... means different things in different places. In Fort Wayne, for example, the wrong crowd meant hanging out with liberal Democrats. In Connecticut, it meant kids who weren't planning to get a PhD from Yale.

Mary Kay Blakely

He is a teenager, after all – a strange agent with holes in his jeans, studs in his ear, a tail down his neck, a cap on his head (backward).

Ellen Karsh

Odours from decaying food wafting through the air when the door is opened, colourful mould growing between a wet gym uniform and the damp carpet underneath, and the complete supply of bath towels scattered throughout the bedroom ...

Barbara Coloroso

From the teenager's perspective, remarriage can feel like a hostile takeover.

Laurence Steinberg and Ann Levine

The trick, which requires the combined skills of a tightrope walker and a cordon bleu chef frying a plain egg, is to take your [pre-teen] daughter seriously without taking everything she says and does every minute seriously.

Stella Chess

One day a [teenage] girl will refer to herself as 'the goddess of social life' and the next day she'll regret that she's the 'ultimate in nerdosity'.

Mary Pipher

There used to be a saying that once your kid got old enough to help around the house, he was no longer around the house to help.

Theresa Bloomingdale

Puberty is the stage children reach that gets parents to start worrying about pregnancy all over again.

Joyce Armor

Oh, to be only half as wonderful as my child thought I was when he was small, and only half as stupid as my teenager now thinks I am.

Rebecca Richards

Teenage girls are extremists who see the world in black-and-white terms, missing shades of grey. Life is either marvellous or not worth living. School is either pure torment or is going fantastically.

Mary Pipher

Hormone Hell

I like to be with my daughter. She's 16 so of course I bore her.

Karen Black

Are you there God? It's me, Margaret. I just told my mother I want a bra. Please help me grow God. You know where. I want to be like everyone else.

Judy Blume

Snow and adolescence are the only problems that disappear if you ignore them long enough.

Earl Wilson

Imagination is something that sits up with dad and mom the first time their teenager stays out late.

Lane Olinghouse

Lately, I can't even look at my mother without wanting to stab her repeatedly.

Angela, My So-Called Life

Well it is every mother's dream to get a good look at her daughter's boyfriend's package.

Roseanne, Roseanne

My teenage son is half man, half mattress.

Val Valentine

Heredity is what makes parents look at their teenage children and question each other.

Barbara Adams

Mothers' Wit

Alligators have the right idea. They eat their young.

Eve Arden

If we spoke to them (our teenagers) in public, they threatened to self-destruct within three minutes.

Erma Bombeck

Mummy's Boy

Few misfortunes can befall a boy which bring worse consequences than to have a really affectionate mother.

Somerset Maugham

The only time a woman really succeeds in changing a man is when he is a baby.

Natalie Wood

Let France have good mothers, and she will have good sons.

Napoleon Bonaparte

The God to whom little boys say their prayers has a face very like their mothers.

James Matthew Barrie

It's been said in the black community that mothers raise their daughters and spoil their sons, they baby them to the point that they don't ever want to leave, give them so much love.

John Singleton

Mother is far too clever to understand anything she does not like.

Arnold Bennett

A boy's best friend is his mother.

Joseph Stefano, Psycho

The male chromosome is an incomplete female chromosome. In other words the male is a walking abortion; aborted at the gene stage. To be male is to be deficient, emotionally limited; maleness is a deficiency disease and males are emotional cripples.

Valerie Solanos

For a woman, a son offers the best chance to know the mysterious male existence.

Carole Klein

The one thing a lawyer won't question is the legitimacy of his mother.

W. C. Fields

A man never sees all that his mother has been to him until it's too late to let her know that he sees it.

W. D. Howells

A young boy said to his mother, 'How old were you when I was born?' His mother replied, 'Twenty-three.' 'Wow, that's a lot of time we missed spending together.'

Anon.

Mothers' Wit

Even a secret agent can't lie to a Jewish mother.

Peter Malkin

Oh, Mother, you go home too early!

Edward Albee, in response to his mother's disbelief of the conversations between the characters in Who's Afraid of Virginia Woolf?

Never throw stones at your mother,
You'll be sorry for it when she's dead,
Never throw stones at your mother,
Throw bricks at your father instead.

Brendan Behan

I am well aware that I am the 'umblest person going … My mother is likewise a very 'umble person. We live in a numble abode.

Uriah Heep in David Copperfield

A triptych in which the presiding deities are Mother, England and Me.

Peter Ackroyd, referring to the memoirs of Noël Coward

Men never recover from the ignorance of their mothers.

Pearl S. Buck

You're not famous until my mother has heard of you.

Jay Leno

The reason a woman knows her son will turn out to be a fine man is that he shows no signs of it.

Anon.

Nothing is quite so horrifying and paralysing as to win the Oedipal struggle and to be awarded your mother as the prize.

Frank Pittman

Many a youngster is much worse than the other boys his mother warns him not to play with.

Anon.

It takes a woman twenty years to make a man of her son, and another woman twenty minutes to make a fool of him.

Helen Rowland

Be a good boy … Hurray and vote for suffrage.

Febb Ensminger Burn, to her son, Henry Thomas Burn. He cast his vote in the Tennessee legislature, breaking a tie and so ratifying women's suffrage

While his mother is alive, a Jewish man will always be a 15-year-old boy.

Anon.

Who's a boy gonna talk to if not his mother?

Donald E. Westlake

A boy is not free to find a partner of his own as long as he must be the partner to his mother.

Frank Pittman

Well behaved: he always speaks as if his mother might be listening.

Mason Cooley

Mothers spend a lifetime excising from their sons the influence of their fathers.

Arthur Lotti

The most powerful ties are the ones to the people who gave us birth … We remain connected, even against our wills.

Anthony Brandt

My mother had to send me to the movies with my birth certificate, so that I wouldn't have to pay the extra fifty cents that the adults had to pay.

Kareem Abdul-Jabar, NBA basketball player

If I were playing third base and my mother were rounding third with the run that was going to beat us, I'd trip her. Oh, I'd pick her up and brush her off and say, 'Sorry, Mom, but nobody beats me.'

Leo Durocher

As the cortege wound slowly along, the queen whispered in a broken voice, 'Here he is,' and I knew that her dry eyes were seeing beyond the coffin a little boy in a sailor suit.

Lady Mabell Airlie, describing Queen Mary watching the funeral procession of her son King George VI

Sooner or later we all quote our mothers.

Bern Williams

Mother love has been much maligned. An over-mothered boy may go through life expecting each new woman to love him the way his mother did. Her love may make any other love seem inadequate.

Frank Pittman

If your mother tells you to do a thing, it is wrong to reply that you won't. It is better and more becoming to intimate that you will do as she bids you, and then afterwards act quietly in the matter according to the dictates of your better judgement.

Mark Twain

We know how powerful our mother was when we were little, but is our wife that powerful to us now? Must we relive our great deed of escape from mama with every other woman in our life?

Frank Pittman

If a man has been his mother's undisputed darling he retains throughout life the triumphant feeling, the confidence in success, which not seldom brings actual success along with it.

Sigmund Freud

I grow more like my mother every day.

W. H. Auden

1946: I go to graduate school at Tulane in order to get distance from a 'possessive' mother. I see a lot of a red-haired girl named Maude-Ellen. My mother asks one day: 'Does Maude-Ellen have warts? Every girl I've known named Maude-Ellen has had warts.' Right: Maude-Ellen had warts.

Bill Bouke

Mothers' Wit

There was never a great man who had not a great mother.

Olive Schreiner

It is not always possible to predict the response of a doting Jewish mother. Witness the occasion on which the late piano virtuoso Oscar Levant telephoned his mother with some important news. He had proposed to his beloved and been accepted. Replied Mother Levant: 'Good, Oscar, I'm happy to hear it. But did you practise today?'

Liz Smith

Why is it every careerist tries to turn his mother into a Madonna – to prove his intellect is a virgin birth, papa had nothing to do with it? It's the sign of the misogynist.

Christina Stead

If that's the world's smartest man, God help us.

Lucille Feynman, talking about her son, a Nobel laureate labelled the world's smartest man by Omni *magazine*

The father is always a Republican toward his son, and his mother's always a Democrat.

Robert Frost

Two of the most difficult tasks a writer can undertake, to write the truth about himself and about his mother.

Time *magazine, on Frank O'Connor's* An Only Child

She is a procession no one can follow after
But be like a little dog following a brass band.

George Barker

Boys are slobs … one reason is that mothers let them get away with it. Mothers are notorious for spoiling male children.

Laura Schlessinger

I look at him and he doesn't look anything like me and I think, am I the mother?

Madonna on her son Rocco

… a boy … reached the age of 6 without ever speaking. One night he suddenly said, 'Please pass the mashed potatoes.' … his mother had always met every one of his needs without him saying a word. This is the epitome of the too good mother.

Elyse Zorn Karlin

Undoubtedly, there are other routes to learning the wishes and dreams of the presumably opposite sex, but I know of none more direct, or more highly motivating, than being the mother of sons.

Mary Kay Blakely

… Fight again and when you come home not another look will you get from me. Not another word. Break your nose, then. Break your mother's heart every time you go from the house.

Mrs Morgan after her son Huw comes home from school having fought a bully in How Green Was My Valley

If Madonna's child is a boy, it'll be the longest relationship she's ever had with a man.

Craig Kilborn

SAMANTHA: Just what the world needs, another man.

Sex in the City, *(Samantha's reaction upon hearing that Miranda has given birth to a boy)*

My birth neither shook the German Empire nor caused much of an upheaval in the home. It pleased mother …

Conrad Veidt

I blame Rousseau, myself. 'Man is born free' indeed. Man is not born free, he is born attached to his mother by a cord and is not capable of looking after himself for at least seven years (seventy in some cases).

Katharine Whitehorn

A man may fight for many things: his country, his principles, his friends, the glistening tear on the cheek of a golden child, but personally I'd mud-wrestle my own mother for a ton of cash, an amusing clock and a sack of French porn.

Blackadder, Blackadder the Third

PHILIP DRUMMOND: Mother gets very impatient if she's kept waiting: I was born three days late; she didn't speak to me for a year.

Diff'rent Strokes

When I was born, my mother mistook the afterbirth as my twin; and the cuter one, too.

Manny Coon, The Kids in the Hall

He had a face only a mother could love … if she was blind in one eye and had that sorta milky film over the other.

Colin Mochrie, Whose Line Is It Anyway?

Men are what their mothers made them.

Ralph Waldo Emerson

Nobody can misunderstand a boy like his own mother.

Norman Douglas

MOTHER: Do you love me. Albert?
ALBERT: Yes
MOTHER: Yes – what?
ALBERT: Yes, please.

Tom Stoppard

The boy's mother had bought him two new ties. He hurried into his bedroom, immediately put on one of them, and hurried back. His mother said, 'What's the matter? You don't like the other one?'

Anon.

There's not a lot of warmth between me and my mother. I asked her about it. I said, 'Mrs Stoller …'

Fred Stoller

All women are bitches except my mother.

Nizar Gabani

SANDY: Since the minute you were born, I knew I would never take another easy breath without knowing you were all right.
SETH: So, I'm like asthma?

The O.C.

I don't care how much of a lama he is, he still needs his mother.

Maria Torres, Spanish woman whose 10-year-old son is believed by Tibetan monks to be a reincarnated lama.

Famous Sons

I wiggle my shoulders, I shake my legs, I walk up and down the stage, I hop around on one foot. But I never bump and grind. I'd never do anything vulgar before an audience. My mother would never allow it.

Elvis Presley

As I have discovered by examining my past, I started out as a child. Coincidentally, so did my brother. My mother did not put all her eggs in one basket, so to speak: she gave me a younger brother named Russell, who taught me what was meant by 'survival of the fittest'.

Bill Cosby

My mother had a great deal of trouble with me, but I think she enjoyed it.

Mark Twain

I was the fattest baby in Clark County, Arkansas. They put me in the newspaper. It was like a prize turnip.

Billy Bob Thornton

When I was a child, my mother said to me, 'If you become a soldier, you'll be a general. If you become a monk you'll end up as the pope.' Instead I became a painter and wound up as Picasso.

Pablo Picasso

My mother loved children – she would have given anything if I had been one.

Groucho Marx

She is my first, great love. She was a wonderful, rare woman – you do not know; as strong, and steadfast, and generous as the sun. She could be as swift as a white whiplash, and as kind and gentle as warm rain, and as steadfast as the irreducible earth beneath us.

D. H. Lawrence

It seems to me that my mother was the most splendid woman I ever knew … I have met a lot of people knocking around the world since, but I have never met a more thoroughly refined woman than my mother. If I have amounted to anything, it will be due to her.

Charles Chaplin

Fifty-four years of love and tenderness and crossness and devotion and unswerving loyalty. Without her I could have achieved a quarter of what I have achieved, not only in terms of success and career, but in terms of personal happiness … She has never stood between me and my life, never tried to hold me too tightly, always let me go free …

Noël Coward

My mother is a walking miracle.

Leonardo DiCaprio

Mothers' Wit

My mother has always been unhappy with what I do. She would rather I do something nicer, like be a bricklayer.

Mick Jagger

It's our money, and we're free to spend it any way we please.

Rose Kennedy, on her son John F. Kennedy's presidential campaign

I've never struck a woman in my life, not even my own mother.

W. C. Fields

He wrote me sad Mother's Day stories. He'd always kill me in the stories and tell me how bad he felt about it. It was enough to bring a tear to a mother's eye.

Connie Zastoupil, mother of Quentin Tarantino

I think of her, two boys dying of tuberculosis, nursing four others … she was a saint.

Richard M. Nixon, on his mother

The things a man has to have are hope and confidence in himself against odds, and sometimes he needs somebody, his pal or his mother or his wife or God, to give him that confidence.

Clark Gable

The whole motivation for any performer is, 'Look at me, Ma!'

Lenny Bruce

You seem to have no real purpose in life and won't realize at the age of 22 that for a man life means work, and hard work if you mean to succeed.

Jennie Jerome Churchill, letter to her son, Winston Churchill

Looking back on my own childhood, after the infant years were over, I do not believe that I ever felt love for any mature person, except my mother …

George Orwell

Hey, Ma, your bad boy did good!

Rocky Graziano, Rocky

Me and My Girl

There came a moment quite suddenly [when] a mother realized that a child was no longer hers … without bothering to ask or even give notice, her daughter had just grown up.

Alice Hoffman

Every bride has to learn it's not her wedding but her mother's.

Saint Augustine

These are my daughters, I suppose. But where in the world did the children vanish?

Phyllis McGinley

As long as a woman can look ten years younger than her own daughter, she is perfectly satisfied.

Oscar Wilde

Republicans are against abortions until their daughters need one. Democrats are for abortion until their daughter wants one.

Grace McGarvie

The mother is only really the mistress of her daughter upon the condition of continually representing herself to her as a model of wisdom and perfection.

Alexandre Dumas Père

A daughter is a little girl who grows up to be a friend.

Anon.

Never grow a wishbone daughter, where your backbone ought to be.

Clementine Paddleford

My mother was very interested in giving her daughters the advantage of music and dance, if we had an interest in it. My father was not.

Suzanne Farrell

If my daughter Liza wants to become an actress, I'll do everything to help her.

Judy Garland

Every mother generally hopes that her daughter will snag a better husband than she managed to do … but she is certain that her boy will never get as good a wife as his father did.

Anon.

A fluent tongue is the only thing a mother don't like her daughter to resemble her in.

Richard Brinsley-Sheridan

How the mother is to be pitied who hath handsome daughters! Locks, bolts, bars, and lectures of morality are nothing to them: they break through them all. They have as much pleasure in cheating a father and mother, as in cheating at cards.

John Gay

Mother, may I go out to swim? Yes my darling daughter. Hang your clothes on a hickory limb, but don't go near the water.

Old proverb

My daughter made me a Jerry Springer watching kit, with crackers, Cheez Whiz, polyester stretch pants and a T-shirt with two fat women fighting over a skinny guy.

Roseanne Barr

I feel better. I feel hornier. I feel more womanly and more accomplished and prouder. [after having her daughter].

Tea Leoni

To me, luxury is to be at home with my daughter, and the occasional massage doesn't hurt.

Olivia Newton-John

A busy mother makes slothful daughters.

Portuguese proverb

I grew up sort of like a princess. I was the baby of the family. I had older brothers, so the little girl always gets everything she wants. As I've gotten older, I've realized that if you want something bad enough, you can have it. I've never gone after something I didn't get. Not yet.

Rachel Bilson

The older I get the more of my mother I see in myself.

Nancy Friday

There is a point when you aren't as much mom and daughter as you are adults and friends. It doesn't happen for everyone – but it did for mom and me.

Jamie Lee Curtis

To my daughter,
Some day daughter, may you have a daughter just like me!
Your mother

Anon.

What do girls do who haven't any mothers to help them through their troubles?

Louisa May Alcott

It is not that I half knew my mother. I knew half of her: the lower half – her lap, legs, feet, her hands and wrists as she bent forward.

Flann O'Brien

A daughter reminds you of all the things you had forgotten about being young. Good and bad.

Maeve O'Reilly

The daughter never ever gives up on the mother, just as the mother never gives up on the daughter. There is a tie there so strong that nothing can break it.

Rachel Billington

There is only one person an English girl hates more than she hates her elder sister; and that is her mother.

George Bernard Shaw

Another way to gain more closet space is to marry off a daughter.

Anon.

A mother worries if her daughter comes home from a date too late – or too early.

Anon.

What the daughter does, the mother did.

Jewish proverb

I have a daughter who goes to SMU. She could've gone to UCLA here in California, but it's one more letter she'd have to remember.

Shecky Greene

Unlike the mother–son relationship, a daughter's relationship with her mother is something akin to bungee diving … there is an invisible emotional cord that snaps her back.

Victoria Secunda

Mothers' Wit

My mother learned that she was carrying me at about the same time the Second World War was declared; with the family talent for magic realism, she once told me she had been to the doctor's on the very day.

Angela Carter

A daughter is a mother's gender partner, her closest ally in the family confederacy …

Victoria Secunda

Mothers are never any good for their daughters. They forget they were just as ugly and silly and scraggy when they were little girls.

Mrs Henrey Robert

Now that you are eighteen
I give you my booty, my spoils,
my Mother & Co. and my ailments.

Anne Sexton

Doesn't that show what an old man I am, when I can say to a mother 'I love your daughter,' and not get the reply 'What are your intentions, and what is your income?'

Lewis Carroll

Generation after generation of women have pledged to raise their daughters differently, only to find that their daughters grow up and fervently pledge the same thing.

Elizabeth Debold

We were the daughters of the post-World War II American dream, the daughters of those idealized fifties sitcom families in which … mother knew her place and a kind of disappointment, and tense, unspoken sexuality rattled around like ice cubes in their nightly cocktails.

Anne Taylor Fleming

Mother always said that I was like a little cricket. Chirping contentedly on the hearth, never able to bear the thought of leaving home.

Beth (Jean Parker) to Jo (Katharine Hepburn), Little Women

… she overshadowed her own daughters … my mother had not the strength to put even some physical distance between them, let alone keep the old monster at emotional arm's length.

Angela Carter, on her maternal grandmother

None but mothers know each other's feelings when we give up our daughters whom we love and cherish so tenderly to the mercies of a man, and perhaps even a stranger.

Emmeline B. Wells

My daughter is every mother's child and every mother is the mother of my child.

Glen Close

Let me see my daughter like my mother could never see me. Let her see me too.

Rebecca Wells

There is only one certainty in the mother–daughter relationship: no matter how hard you try, mother will make mistakes and daughter will too, but the mistakes daughter makes will probably be all 'mother's fault'.

Faith Ringgold

With my poems, I finally won even my mother. The longest wooing of my life.

Marge Piercy

Janie works hard, of course, and she's a good wife and mother, but do you know she's never once made a gingerbread house with her children?

Mildred Hastings, speaking about Jane Eagen, her daughter (a successful insurance broker and mother of three)

From afar I can believe my family loves me fundamentally. They only say, 'When fishing for treasures in the flood, be careful not to pull in girls,' because that is what one says about daughters.

Maxine Hong Kingston

The Depression era generation of mothers … believed … the worst fate was to be independent. Their daughters, jolted by Vietnam, the sexual revolution, and feminism, were largely committed to themselves. For them, the worst fate was to be dependent.

Victoria Secunda

[My daughter] says she wants to marry a rich man, so she can have a Porsche. My rejoinder always is: 'Go out and get rich yourself, so you can buy your own.'

Carol Royce

Oh my son's my son till he gets him a wife,
But my daughter's my daughter all her life.

Dinah Maria Mulock Craik

Of all the haunting moments of motherhood, few rank with hearing your own words come out of your daughter's mouth.

Victoria Secunda

Where does a mother end and a daughter begin?

White Oleander

A stubborn daughter cannot be bought – though she can be bribed with ice cream.

Anon.

[This is to explain] just how your mom turned out to be the kind of hairpin she is.

Carole Burnett, note to her daughters

The only other person I've apologized to is my mother and that was court ordered.

Karen, Will and Grace

Mother, just because I wear trackies and play sports *does not make me a lesbian*!

Jules, Bend It Like Beckham

THELMA CATES: You're my child!
JESSIE CATES: I'm what became of your child!

Night, Mother

My daughter thinks I'm nosy. At least that's what she says in her diary.

Sally Poplin

So I'm licking jelly off my boyfriend, right, and all of a sudden I'm thinking, 'Oh my God, I'm turning into my mother.'

Sarah Silverman

Having It All Working Mums

Being a child at home alone in the summer is a high-risk occupation. If you call your mother at work thirteen times an hour, she can hurt you.

Erma Bombeck

I think we're seeing in working mothers a change from 'Thank God it's Friday' to, 'Thank God it's Monday.' If any working mother has not experienced that feeling, her children are not adolescent.

Ann Diehl

Touring full-time with children is a study in sleep deprivation: the day never ends! Many times on the road we do a sound check, then everybody goes to dinner. If I'm eating with the kids, I go back to my dressing room and fall into a dead sleep until it's time for me to get up and put my stage clothes on.

Amy Grant

Any sane person would have left long ago. But I cannot. I have my sons.

Princess Diana

I love what used to be called women's work. When women make quilts or something like that, it was something they could pick up or put down, and go back to after they start dinner or weed the garden or whatever … feed the baby. I like that. I liked knowing where I was going to be for a while.

Chuck Close

I've yet to be on a campus where most women weren't worrying about some aspect of combining marriage, children, and a career. I've yet to find one where many men were worrying about the same thing.

Gloria Steinem

In their 30s women really start to live … they're not children any more, and they're not just mothers.

Kelly Lynch

Being a full-time mother is one of the highest salaried jobs … since the payment is pure love.

Mildred B. Vermont

There are 80 million moms in the United States. Forty million stay at home with their children.

Andrew Shue

All mothers are working mothers.

Anon.

A growing number of young women who have the freedom to decide have decided that career can wait, and the delicious early years of their children's lives can't.

Suzanne Fields

At work you think of the children you have left at home. At home you think of the work you've left unfinished. Such a struggle is unleashed within yourself. Your heart is rent.

Golda Meir

What is sad for women of my generation is that they weren't supposed to work if they had families. What were they going to do when the children are grown – watch the raindrops coming down the window pane?

Jackie Kennedy

The men who still have the largest share of the power in society don't do any domestic work. The very people who are making our most important decisions should know how to cook, know how to grow a garden, diaper a baby, and raise young people. They should not only know these things but practise them.

Susan Griffin

No book has yet been written in praise of a woman who let her husband and children starve or suffer while she invented even the most useful things, or wrote books, or expressed herself in art, or evolved philosophic systems.

Anna Garlin Spencer

I will always have a career. I believe in working. I don't believe that taking care of your house and children is enough for a woman. You don't feel complete.

Joan Chen

I just decided that I would not put my professional life on hold to raise children. I know that sounds selfish to a lot of people and I don't know if what I'm doing is the right thing. But that's the way I'm doing it.

Emmanuelle Beart

Were women meant to do everything – work and have babies?

Candice Bergen

The phrase 'working mother' is redundant.

Jane Sellman

I have a brain and a uterus, and I use both.

Patricia Schroeder, US Congresswoman, on being an elected official and a mother

She was – but I assure you that she was a very bad cook.

Louis Adolphe Thiers, after someone had questioned his social status, commenting that his mother had been a cook

Don't tell my mother I'm in politics. She thinks I play piano in a whorehouse.

American saying from the Depression

The world is full of women blindsided by the unceasing demands of motherhood, still flabbergasted by how a job can be terrific and tortuous.

Anna Quindlen

But while being a mother is admittedly a lifelong preoccupation, it cannot, should not, must not be a lifelong occupation.

Melinda M. Marshall

After your baby is born, guilt can grow into a monster that sits on your shoulder and whispers into your ear, 'Mirror, mirror on the wall who's the guiltiest of them all?' The answer is working mothers.

Jean Marzollo

If your children look up to you, you've made a success of life's biggest job.

Anon.

I am my kid's mom.

Dr Laura Schlessinger

'Working mother' is a misnomer … It implies that any mother without a definite career is lolling around eating bon-bons, reading novels, and watching soap opera.

Liz Smith

Q: What would have made a family and career easier for you?
A: Being born a man.

Anon.

It's only too easy to idealize a mother's job. We know well that every job has its frustrations and its boring routines and its times of being the last thing anyone would choose to do. Well, why shouldn't the care of babies and children be thought of that way too?

D. W. Winnicott

I can remember no time when I did not understand that my mother must write books because people would have and read them; but I cannot remember one hour in which her children needed her and did not find her.

Elizabeth Stuart Phelps

... a business career for a woman and her need for a woman's life as wife and mother, are not enemies at all, unless we make them so.

Hortense Odlum

I was standing in the schoolyard waiting for a child when another mother came up to me. 'Have you found work yet?' she asked. 'Or are you still just writing?'

Anne Tyler

She isn't harassed. She's busy, and it's glamorous to be busy ... very like the glamorous image of the busy top executive ... [this analogy] obscures the wage gap between them at work, and their different amounts of backstage support at home.

Arlie Hochschild

Clearly, society has a tremendous stake in insisting on a woman's natural fitness for the career of mother: the alternatives are all too expensive.

Ann Oakley

I do not want to be covetous, but I think I speak the minds of many a wife and mother when I say ... [I] have worked hard for twenty-five years and have never known what it was to receive a financial compensation and to have what was really my own.

Emma Watrous

If you would shut your door against the children for an hour a day and say: 'Mother is working on her five-act tragedy in blank verse!' you would be surprised how they would respect you. They would probably all become playwrights.

Brenda Ueland

If work is part of your identity, think very carefully before you give it up.

Jean Marzollo

Nagging guilt is like grey paint splashed over life's sparkling moments.

Sally Shannon

Women who bear children before they establish serious habits of work, may never establish them at all.

Erica Jong

Career mothers are not kidding anybody. Being a mom is the hardest job of all. You got to work to rest.

Sandy Duncan

One of my children wrote in a third grade piece on how her mother spent her time, 'one-half time on home, one-half time on outside things, one-half time writing'.

Charlotte Montgomery

When you're sitting at home with sick all over your nightie, it's great to be able to do something which means you don't have to go out.

Jo Brand, on writing her first book

I have often felt that I cheated my children a little. I was never so totally theirs as most mothers are. I gave to audiences what belonged to my children, got back from audiences the love my children longed to give me.

Eleanor Roosevelt

It's an old trick now, God knows, but it works every time. At the very moment women start to expand their place in the world, scientific studies deliver compelling reasons for them to stay home.

Mary Kay Blakely

When you combine wife, mother, career and all, each role becomes the perfect excuse for avoiding the worst aspects of the other.

Bettina Arndt

I'm tired of earning my own living, paying my own bills, raising my own child … Self-sufficiency is exhausting. Autonomy is lonely. It's so hard to be a feminist if you are a woman.

Jane O'Reilly

I have spent so long erecting partitions around the part of me that writes – learning how to close the door on it when ordinary life intervenes, how to close the door on ordinary life when it's time to start writing again – that I'm not sure I could fit the two parts of me back together now.

Anne Tyler

At home, it was cooking, cleaning, taking care of the kids, going to PTA, Girl Scouts. But when I got into the office, everything was different, I was different.

Estelle Shuster

My job is quite suitable for full-time mothering.

Mare Winningham

Take motherhood: nobody ever thought of putting it on a moral pedestal until some brash feminists pointed out, about a century ago, that the pay is lousy and the career ladder non-existent.

Barabara Ehrenreich

It's hard being a working mum, but we have fun. We do shows together. We play all the parts in *The Wizard of Oz*. She watches the show, and does imitations of Julie Kavner.

Tracey Ullman

Adults are always asking kids what they want to be when they grow up because they are looking for ideas.

Paula Poundstone

EDINA: Oooh, sweetie … darling … oh god, sweetie what a day, what a day I've had sweetie, darling. (*Throws herself down on kitchen table*) I have been at work since I left here this morning!
SAFFY: You want some lunch?

Absolutely Fabulous

Aspirational Mums

Mothers all want their sons to grow up to be president, but they don't want them to become politicians in the process.

John F. Kennedy

All mothers think their children are oaks, but the world never lacks for cabbages.

Robertson Davies

I want my children to have all the things I couldn't afford. Then I want to move in with them.

Phyllis Diller

Only mothers can think of the future, because they give birth to it in their children.

Maxim Gorky

The mother nourishes the foetus in the womb, hoping for a son, who will grow and earn and give her money to enjoy herself.

Sri Guru Granth Sahib

The mother loves her child most divinely, not when she surrounds him with comfort and anticipates his wants, but when she resolutely holds him to the highest standards and is content with nothing less than his best.

Hamilton Wright Mabie

Mama exhorted her children at every opportunity to 'Jump at de sun'. We might not land on the sun, but at least we would get off the ground.

Zora Neale Hurston

One woman will brag about her children, while another complains about hers; they could probably swap children without swapping tunes.

Anon.

If I have children I am going to make sure people don't ask them, 'Are you going to be an actor?' My mother said I could be anything I wanted except a policeman.

Kate Beckinsale

Thank you to Martin Scorsese – I hope my son will marry your daughter.

Cate Blanchett

My mother was against me being an actress until I introduced her to Frank Sinatra.

Angie Dickinson

My mother wanted me to be her wings, to fly as she never quite had the courage to do. I love her for that. I love the fact that she wanted to give birth to her own wings.

Erica Jong

I doubt if a charging elephant, or a rhino, is as determined or as hard to check as a socially ambitious mother.

Will Rogers

It's a rare parent who can see his or her child clearly and objectively. At a school board meeting I attended … the only definition of a gifted child on which everyone in the audience could agree was 'mine'.

Jane Adams

One day my mother called me … and she said, 'Forty-nine million Americans saw you on television tonight. One of them is the father of my future grandchild, but he's never going to call you because you wore your glasses.'

Lesley Stahl, newsreader.

Every beetle is a gazelle in the eyes of its mother.

Arab proverb

I would be most content if my children grew up to be the kind of people who think decorating consists mostly of building enough bookshelves.

Anna Quindlen

My mom wanted to be an actress, so she figured her son could be one for her. She said she'd give me $100 to take drama instead of home ec. – I wanted to be a cook like my pops.

Tobey Maguire

My mother married a very good man … and she is not at all keen on my doing the same.

George Bernard Shaw

Perhaps I can be of assistance. My mother says that I have an IQ that rivals that of Alfred Einstein.

Rick, 15/Love

Dr French: You're just one step away from plain white trash, aren't you Jennifer? Your mother was a biology teacher in Cheshire; you used to sit there on your white pony and you'd dream … of getting all the way … to the BBC.

French and Saunders

Youth fades; love droops; the leaves of friendship fall; a mother's secret hope outlives them all.

Oliver Wendell Holmes Jr

Dare to be Different

Unconventional Families

You hear a lot of dialogue on the death of the American family. Families aren't dying. They're merging into big conglomerates.

Erma Bombeck

What is free time? I'm a single mother. My free moments are filled with loving my little girl.

Roma Downey

Single women have a dreadful propensity for being poor. Which is one very strong argument in favour of matrimony.

Jane Austen

Yes, single-parent families are different from two-parent families. And urban families are different from rural ones, and families with six kids and a dog are different from one-child, no-pet households. But even if there is only one adult presiding at the dinner table, yours is every bit as much a real family as the Waltons.

Marge Kennedy

A widow has two duties of a contradictory nature – she is a mother and she ought to exert a father's power.

Honoré de Balzac

It's important for all single parents to remember that not everything that goes wrong, from your son's bad attitude towards school to the six holes in your teenage daughter's ear, is because you live in a single-parent home. Every family has its problems.

Marge Kennedy

As complicated as joint custody is, it allows the delicious contradiction of having children and maintaining the intimacy of life-before-kids.

Delia Ephron

Your basic extended family today includes your ex-husband or -wife, your ex's new mate, your new mate, possibly your new mate's ex and any new mate that your new mate's ex has acquired.

Delia Ephron

There is nothing to suggest that mothering cannot be shared by several people.

H. R. Schaffer

People talk about dysfunctional families; I've never seen any other kind.

Sue Grafton

That's the only good thing about divorce. You get to sleep with your mother.

Anita Loos

MIRANDA: Well, I got pregnant, became a single mother, and stopped having any time to eat.

Sex in the City *(Miranda explains how she can now fit into her 'skinny jeans')*

'If only I had a wife!' I used to think, 'who could stay home and keep the children happy, why I could support six of them. A cinch.'

Brenda Ueland, a divorced working mother

I worry about people who get born nowadays, because they get born into such tiny families – sometimes into no family at all. When you're the only pea in the pod, your parents are likely to get you confused with the Hope Diamond.

Russell Baker

You can be much more alone with other people than you are by yourself. Even if it's people you love.

Philip Dunne and Joseph L. Mankiewicz

Adopted kids are such a pain. You have to teach them how to look like you.

Gilda Radnor

It helps when I can send my daughters off to their father's so I can support my new book with a national publicity tour. I started writing the book when my daughter was five. It took me almost four years.

Meg Tilly

I married Nicholas Ray, the director. People yawned. Later on I married his son, and from the press's reaction – you'd have thought I was committing incest or robbing the cradle!

Gloria Grahame

In a broken nest there are few whole eggs.

Chinese proverb

When you have a good mother and no father, God kind of sits in. It's not enough, but it helps.

Dick Gregory

The Birds Have Flown

It kills you to see them grow up. But I guess it would kill you quicker if they didn't.

Barbara Kingsolver

The best way to keep children at home is to make the home atmosphere pleasant, and let the air out of the tyres.

Dorothy Parker

No matter how old a mother is, she watches her middle-aged children for signs of improvement.

Florida Scott-Maxwell

The successful mother sets her children free and becomes more free herself in the process.

Robert Havighurst

I take a very practical view of raising children, I put a sign in each of their rooms: checkout time is eighteen years.

Erma Bombeck

Most children threaten to run away from home. This is the only thing that keeps some parents going.

Phyllis Diller

You see much more of your children once they leave home.

Lucille Ball

If your children spend most of their time in other people's houses, you're lucky; if they all congregate at your house, you're blessed.

Mignon McLaughlin

Until I got married, when I used to go out, my mother said goodbye to me as though I was emigrating.

Thora Hird

Nothing looks as lonely as your mom before she sees you coming up the platform.

Pam Brown

Mothers need transfusions fairly often – phone calls, letters, bright postcards from the Outer Hebrides.

Heulwen Roberts

A mother never realizes that her children are no longer children.

Holbrook Jackson

If a woman's role in life is limited solely to housewife/ mother, it clearly ends when she can no longer bear children and the children she has borne leave home.

Betty Friedan

I thought it would be horrible when they got married and left … But that's silly you know. By the time they grow up … they're not the same little kids and you're not the same mother … and you're ready.

Anonymous mother

Lonesome? God, no! … After all those years … you finally get to the point where you want to scream: 'Fall out of the nest already, you guys, will you? It's time.'

Anonymous mother of four

Hello, Arthur. This is your mother. Do you remember me? … Someday you'll get married and have children of your own and, honey, when you do, I only pray that they'll make you suffer the way you're making me. That's a mother's prayer.'

Mike Nichols

I became the butterfly. I got out of the cocoon, and I flew.

Lynn Redgrave, describing leaving home and moving to California

When mothers talk about the depression of the empty nest, they're not mourning the passing of all those wet towels on the floor, or the music that numbs your teeth, or even the bottle of capless shampoo dribbling down the shower drain. They're upset because they've gone from supervisor of a child's life to a spectator. It's like being the vice president of the United States.

Erma Bombeck

Kids are cute, babies are cute, puppies are cute. The little things are cute. See, nature did this on purpose so that we would want to take care of our young. Made them cute, tricked us. Then gradually they get older and older, until one day your mother sits you down and says, 'You know, I think you're ugly enough to get your own apartment.'

Cathy Ladman

After they've gone what you miss most is the noise.

Anon.

I'm sorry I scared you mother. It was a simple, run-of-the-mill orgasm.

Nikki, Spin City

Anyone for Botox?
Mums on Ageing

Women over 50 don't have babies because they would put them down and forget where they left them.

Anon.

The woman who tells her age is either too young to have anything to lose or too old to have anything to gain.

Chinese proverb

One of the many things nobody ever tells you about middle age is that it's such a nice change from being young.

Dorothy Canfield Fisher

The really frightening thing about middle age is knowing you'll grow out of it.

Doris Day

Only in America do these peasants, our mothers, get their hair dyed platinum at the age of 60, and walk up and down Collins Avenue in Florida in pedal pushers and mink stoles – and with opinions on every subject under the sun. It isn't their fault they were given a gift like speech – look, if cows could talk, they would say things just as idiotic.

Philip Roth

I refuse to admit that I am more than 52, even if that does make my sons illegitimate.

Nancy Astor

We are always the same age inside.

Gertrude Stein

Thirty-five is when you finally get your head together and your body starts falling apart.

Caryn Leschen

Maybe it's true that life begins at 50 ... but everything else starts to wear out, fall out or spread out.

Phyllis Diller

You're never too old to grow up.

Shirley Conran

Mothers are inclined to feel limp at 50. This is because the children have taken most of her stuffing to build their nests.

Samantha Armstrong

Wrinkles are hereditary. Parents get them from their children.

Mae West

There is no more creative force in the world than the menopausal woman with zest.

Margaret Mead

Old age ain't no place for sissies.

Bette Davis

I refuse to think of them as chin hairs. I think of them as stray eyebrows.

Janette Barber

Anyone for Botox?

Old age is like a plane flying through a storm. Once you're aboard, there's nothing you can do.

Golda Meir

When you made a face and your mother said, 'Be careful your face might freeze that way,' she was right. It just takes longer than you think.

Johanna Newell

I have flabby thighs, but fortunately my stomach covers them.

Joan Rivers

I don't plan to grow old gracefully. I plan to have face lifts until my ears meet.

Rita Rudner

At 50 you have the choice of keeping your face or your figure, and it's much better to keep your face.

Barbara Cartland

You know, mother, it's good to see that age hasn't slowed down your sarcasm, regardless of what it's done to your body.

Dot, High Society

Every time I think I'm getting old and gradually going to the grave, something else happens.

Lillian Carter

Wisdom doesn't automatically come with old age. Nothing does – except wrinkles.

Abigail Van Buren

Grandmas

If your baby is beautiful and perfect, never cries or fusses, sleeps on schedule and burps on demand, an angel all the time, you're the grandma.

Theresa Bloomingdale

Why do grandparents and grandchildren get along so well? They have the same enemy –the mother.

Claudette Colbert

It's funny that those things your kids did that got on your nerves seem so cute when your grandchildren do them.

Anon.

Just about the time she thinks her work is done, she becomes a grandmother.

Edward H. Dreschnack

You do not really understand something unless you can explain it to your grandmother.

Proverb

When a child is born, so are grandmothers.

Judith Levy

My grandmother was a very tough woman. She buried three husbands and two of them were just napping.

Rita Rudner

We have become a grandmother.

Margaret Thatcher

What in heaven's name is strange about a grandmother dancing nude? I'll bet lots of grandmothers do it.

Sally Rand

My grandmother is over 80 and still doesn't need glasses. Drinks right out of the bottle.

Henry Youngman

When my grandson asked me how old I was, I teasingly replied, 'I'm not sure.' 'Look in your underwear Grandma,' he advised. 'Mine says I'm four.'

Anon.

When my 3-year-old son opened the birthday gift from his grandma, he discovered a water pistol. He squealed with delight and headed for the nearest sink. I was not so pleased. I turned to mum and said, 'I'm surprised at you. Don't you remember how we used to drive you crazy with water guns?' Mum smiled and then replied … 'I remember.'

Anon.

The simplest toy, one which even the youngest child can operate, is called a grandparent.

Sam Levenson

The best place to be when you're sad is your grandma's lap.

Jeannie, aged 7

If you want something expensive ask your grandma.

Matthew, aged 12

My grandma can say more in a sentence than a college professor can say in an hour and a half.

Angela, aged 14

A grandmother pretends she doesn't know who you are on Halloween

Erma Bombeck

Becoming a grandmother is wonderful. One moment you're just a mother. The next you are all wise and prehistoric.

Pam Brown

Being pretty on the inside means you don't hit your brother and you eat up all your peas – that's what my grandma taught me.

Lord Chesterfield

Grandchildren don't make a man feel old; it's the knowledge he's married to a grandmother.

G. Norman Collie

If you want to civilize a man begin with his grandmother.

Victor Hugo

It is as grandmothers that our mothers come into the fulness of their grace. When a man's mother holds his children in her gladden arms he is aware of the roundness of life's cycle; of the mystic harmony of life's ways.

Christopher Morley

Truth be told, being a grandma is as close as we ever get to perfection. The ultimate warm sticky bun with plump raisins and nuts. Clouds nine, ten and eleven.

Bryna Nelson Paston

If nothing is going well call your grandmother.

Italian proverb

If becoming a grandmother was only a matter of choice, I should advise every one of you straight away to become one. There is no fun for old people like it.

Hannah Whithall Smith

It's such a good thing to be a mother of a mother – that's why the world calls her grandmother.

Anon.

A grandmother is a babysitter who watches the kids instead of television.

Anon.

Grandmas are mums with lots of frosting.

Anon.

Grandmas are people who take delight in hearing babies breathing into the telephone.

Anon.

Grandmothers are good at sitting on the floor to play, but they can be terribly difficult to get upright again.

Anon.

Grandmas never run out of hugs or cookies.

Anon.

Grandmothers are just antique little girls.

Anon.

Grandmother – a wonderful mother with lots of practice.

Anon.

The old-time mother who used to wonder where her boy was now has a grandson who wonders where his mother is.

Kin Hubbard

If a tie is like kissing your sister, losing is like kissing your grandmother with her teeth out.

George Brett

When the grandmothers of today hear the word 'Chippendales', they don't necessarily think of chairs.

Jean Kerr

It was dramatic to watch my grandmother decapitate a turkey with an axe the day before Thanksgiving. Nowadays the expense of hiring grandmothers for the axe work would probably qualify all turkeys so honoured with 'gourmet' status.

Russell Baker

Infant undershirts were made to keep grandmothers happy on those chilly ninety-degree days in mid-August.

Linda Fiterman

My grandmothers are full of memories. Smelling of soap and onions and wet clay. With veins rolling roughly over quick hands. They have many clean words to say.

Margaret Walker

Her grandmother, as she gets older, is not fading but rather becoming more concentrated.

Paulette Bates Alden

A grandmother is a mother who has a second chance.

Anon.

You have to stay in shape. My grandmother, she started walking five miles a day when she was 60. She's 97 today and we don't know where the hell she is.

Ellen DeGeneres

Keep grandmas off the streets … legalize bingo.

Car bumper sticker

A mother becomes a true grandmother the day she stops noticing the terrible things her children do because she is so enchanted with the wonderful things her grandchildren do.

Lois Wyse

Soon I will be an old, white-haired lady, into whose lap someone places a baby, saying 'Smile, Grandma!' I, who myself was so recently photographed on my grandmother's lap.

Liv Ullmann

It is remarkable how, overnight, a quiet mature lady can learn to sit cross-legged on the floor and play a tin drum, quack like a duck, sing all the verses of 'The Twelve Days of Christmas', make paper flowers, draw pigs, and sew on the ears of severely injured teddy bears.

Anon.

Grandma knows best, but no one ever listens.

Mary McBride

My grandmother died before teabags. I am grateful. My mother never admitted their existence.

M. F. K. Fisher

A grandmother will put a sweater on you when she is cold, feed you when she is hungry, and put you to bed when she is tired.

Erma Bombeck

Your sons weren't made to like you. That's what grandchildren were for!

Jane Smiley

The proliferation of support groups suggests to me that too many Americans are growing up in homes that do not contain a grandmother. A home without a grandmother is like an egg without salt and Helpists know it.

Florence King

One of life's greatest mysteries is how the boy who wasn't good enough to marry your daughter can be the father of the smartest grandchild in the world

Jewish proverb

My grandmother wanted to live long enough to vote for a woman president. I'll be satisfied if I live to see a woman go before the Supreme Court and hear the justices acknowledge, 'Gentlemen, she's human. She deserves the protection of our laws.'

Martha Wright Griffiths

Maybe there is no actual place called hell. Maybe hell is just having to listen to our grandmothers breathe through their noses when they're eating sandwiches.

Jim Carrie

War and Peas
Mums, Menus and Mealtimes

I do not like broccoli and I haven't liked it since I was a little kid and my mother made me eat it. Now I am President of the United States and I am not going to eat any more broccoli.

George Bush

Even today, well-brought-up English girls are taught by their mothers to boil all veggies for at least a month and a half, just in case one of the dinner guests turns up without his teeth.

Calvin Trillin

My mother's menu consisted of two choices: take it or leave it.

Buddy Hackett

Mothers' Wit

Ask your child what he wants for dinner only if he is buying.

Fran Lebowitz

In general my children refuse to eat anything that hasn't danced on television.

Erma Bombeck

When my mother had to get dinner for eight she'd just make enough for sixteen and only serve half.

Gracie Allen

My mother was a good recreational cook, but what she basically believed about cooking was that if you worked hard and prospered, someone else would do it for you.

Nora Ephron

The most remarkable thing about my mother is that for thirty years she served the family nothing but leftovers. The original meal has never been found.

Calvin Trillin

A mother is a person who, seeing there are only four pieces of pie for five people, promptly announces she never did care for pie.

Tenneva Jordan

My cooking was so bad my kids thought Thanksgiving was to commemorate Pearl Harbor.

Phyllis Diller

I come from a family where gravy is considered a beverage.

Erma Bombeck

A food is not necessarily essential just because your child hates it.

Katharine Whitehorn

Thanksgiving dinners take eighteen hours to prepare. They are consumed in twelve minutes. Half times take twelve minutes. This is no coincidence.

Erma Bombeck

The age of your children is a key factor in how quickly you are served in a restaurant. We once had a waiter in Canada who said, 'Could I get you your check?' and we answered, 'How about the menu first?'

Erma Bombeck

I don't even butter my bread; I consider that cooking.

Katherine Cebrian

Most turkeys taste better the day after; my mother's tasted better the day before.

Rita Rudner

I hope you all saved room, because I made your favourite dessert. Store-bought snack cakes – both kinds.

Marge, The Simpsons

I was born because my mother needed a fourth for meals.

Beatrice Lille

It's bizarre that the produce manager is more important to my children's health than the paediatrician.

Meryl Streep

No matter what my mum does to it, spinach always tastes awful.

Kelly, aged 9

My family can always tell when I'm well into a novel because the meals get very crummy.

Anne Tyler

Chicken soup: an ancient miracle drug containing equal parts of erythromycin, cocaine, interferon and TLC. The only ailment chicken soup can't cure is neurotic dependence on one's mother.

Arthur Naiman

I thought how mothers feed their babies with tiny little spoons and forks, so I wondered, What do Chinese mothers use? Toothpicks?

George Carlin

When mother's relatives visited, delicacies were cooked. When father's guest arrrived, mother swelled and had a fit.

Punjabi proverb

As a mother I am often confused … One day I tell them to eat what they like, their bodies know intuitively what they need; and the next I say, 'OK, that's it – no more junk food in this house!'

Martha Boesing

Early on, we equate being a good parent with how we feed our children. You're a 'good mother' if you feed your kid food that is healthy.

Goldie Alfasi

If you have enough butter, anything is good.

Julia Childs

I refuse to believe that trading recipes is silly. Tuna fish casserole is at least as real as corporate stock.

Barbara Harrison

Even while I protest the assembly-line production of our food, our songs, our language, and eventually our souls, I know that it was a rare home that baked good bread in the old days. Mother's cooking was with rare exceptions poor.

John Steinbeck

And, indeed, is there not something holy about a great kitchen? … the range like an altar … before which my mother bowed in perpetual homage, a fringe of sweat upon her upper lip and the fire glowing in her cheeks.

Angela Carter

My kids keep trying to convince me that there are two separate parts of their stomachs, one dedicated to dinner and the other to dessert.

Anna Quindlen

My mother cooked with reckless abandon.

Anon.

This a kitchen, not a maternity ward: cakes are delivered here; cakes and other disasters!

Ben Parkinson

I know how hard it is for you to put food on your family.

George W. Bush

In childhood memories of every good cook, there's a large kitchen, a warm stove, a simmering pot and a mom.

Barbara Costikyan

Life is too short to stuff a mushroom.

Shirley Conran

How to eat like a child: divide spinach into little piles. Rearrange again into new piles. After five or six manoeuvres, sit back and say you are full.

Delia Ephron

For a long time I thought coq au vin meant love in a lorry.

Victoria Wood

Mothers routinely cook eggs, bacon and waffles for their family every morning, even though their husband and children never have time to eat it.

Anon.

Carrots do something for children's vision. Kids can spot carrots no matter how you disguise them.

Anon.

Mother's Little Helper
Mums on Prozac

Insanity is my only means of relaxation.

Anon.

A friend of mine confused her Valium with her birth control pills. She has fourteen kids but she doesn't really care.

Anon.

All of us have moments in our lives that test our courage. Taking children into a house with a white carpet is one of them.

Erma Bombeck

The worker can unionize, go out on strike; mothers are divided from each other in homes, tied to their children by compassionate bonds; our wildcat strikes have most often taken the form of physical or mental breakdown.

Adrienne Rich

The statistics on sanity are that one out of every four Americans are suffering from some form of mental illness. Think of your three best friends. If they're OK then it's you.

Rita Mae Brown

Know that every mother occasionally feels 'at the end of her rope'. When you reach the end of your rope, don't add guilt to your frustration. No one said motherhood was going to be easy.

Heather King

Mothers are all slightly insane.

J. D. Salinger

Children are the anchors that hold a mother to life.

Sophocles

I believe that always, or almost always, in all childhoods and in all the lives that follow them, the mother represents madness. Our mothers always remain the strangest, craziest people we've ever met.

Marguerite Duras

> 'It's so sweet to hear their chatter, watch them grow
>   and thrive,'
> she says to his departing smile. Then, nursing
> the youngest child, sits staring at her feet.
> To the wind she says, 'They have eaten me alive.'

Gwen Harwood

Be it ever so humble there's no place like home for sending one slowly crackers.

Anon.

Don't be afraid of me because I'm coming back from the mental hospital – I'm your mother.

Allen Ginsberg

I used to be excellent. Since having a baby I couldn't tell you what day it is.

Gwyneth Paltrow

What we choose to call sanity is a big house where the bad have no mothers.

The Clown Prince of Darkness

When women reach the age of maturity, Mother Nature sometimes overworks their frustration to the point of irrationalism.

Mark Hanna, Nathan Hertz, Dr Von Loeb

I tried to commit suicide by sticking my head in the oven, but there was a cake in it.

Lesley Boone

Delusions are often functional. A mother's opinions about her children's beauty, intelligence, goodness, et cetera ad nauseum, keep her from drowning them at birth.

Lazarus Long

I'm trying very hard to understand this generation. They have adjusted the timetable for childbearing so that menopause and teaching a 16-year-old how to drive a car will occur in the same week.

Erma Bombeck

If Mr Vincent Price were to be co-starred with Miss Bette Davis in a story by Mr Edgar Allan Poe directed by Mr Roger Corman, it could not fully express the pent-up violence and depravity of a single day in the life of the average family.

Quentin Crisp

Mothers' Wit

This is Dr Niles Crane, filling in for my ailing brother, Dr Frasier Crane. Although I feel perfectly qualified to fill Frasier's radio shoes, I should warn you that while Frasier is a Freudian, I am a Jungian. So there'll be no blaming Mother today.

Niles, Frasier

My mother's crazy, that's why I had her committed. Well, she's not crazy so much as she really bugs me … yeah, she's a bitch.

Karen, Will and Grace

LAWYER: She had three children, right?
WITNESS: Yes.
LAWYER: How many were boys?
WITNESS: None.
LAWYER: Were there girls?

Genuine courtroom transcript

Reality is just a crutch for people who can't cope with drugs.

Lily Tomlin

She used to eat chops in the small hours and sleep in a hat. Once she arrived home at 7 a.m. carrying a gate. Who am I to say there was anything wrong with her?

Alan Coren

My mom was a little weird. When I was little she would make chocolate frosting. And she'd let me lick the beaters. And then she'd turn them off.

Marty Cohen

If you want to ask about my drug problem, go ask my big, fat, smart, ten-pound daughter, she'll answer any questions you have about it.

Courtney Love

In raising my kids, I have lost my mind but found my soul.

Lisa T. Shepherd

A Dirty Job, but Someone's Got to Do It! Housework

Cleaning your house while the kids are still growing is like shovelling the walk before it stops snowing.

Phyllis Diller

My theory on housework is, if the item doesn't multiply, smell, catch fire, or block the refrigerator door, let it be. No one else cares. Why should you?

Erma Bombeck

My mother was an authority on pigsties. 'This is the worst-looking pigsty I have ever seen in my life and I want it cleaned up right now!'

Bill Cosby

How do you know it's time to wash the dishes and clean your house? Look inside your pants. If you find a penis in there, it's not time.

Jo Brand

Housework is something that you do that nobody notices unless you haven't done it.

Sam Ewing

When it comes to housework the one thing no book of household management can ever tell you is how to begin. Or maybe I mean why.

Katharine Whitehorn

My idea of superwoman is someone who scrubs her own floors.

Bette Midler

My second favourite household chore is ironing. My first being hitting my head on the top bunk until I faint.

Erma Bombeck

I think housework is the reason most women go to the office.

Heloise Cruse

I am thankful for a lawn that needs mowing, windows that need cleaning and gutters that need fixing because it means I have a home … I am thankful for the piles of laundry and ironing because it means my loved ones are nearby.

Nancie J. Carmody

Nature abhors a vacuum. And so do I.

Anne Gibbons

A Dirty Job, but Someone's Got to Do It!

Don't cook. Don't clean. No man will ever make love to a woman because she waxed the linoleum – 'My God, the floor's immaculate. Lie down you hot bitch.'

Joan Rivers

The Rose Bowl is the only bowl I've ever seen that I didn't have to clean.

Erma Bombeck

Housework can't kill you, but why take a chance?

Phyllis Diller

I hate housework! You make the beds, you do the dishes – and six months later you have to start all over again.

Joan Rivers

Any mother could perform the jobs of several air-traffic controllers with ease.

Lisa Alther

A house does not need a wife any more than it needs a husband.

Charlotte Perkins Gilman

Neurotics build castles in the air, psychotics live in them. My mother cleans them.

Rita Rudner

If I'm sitting on the toilet and I'm looking at the grouting on the tiles, that grouting really gets me. Mothers have a thing about grouting.

Sharon Osbourne

There's something wrong with a mother who washes out a measuring cup with soap and water after she's only measured water in it.

Erma Bombeck

Housework is a treadmill from futility to oblivion with stop-offs at tedium and counter-productivity.

Erma Bombeck

My idea of housework is to sweep the room with a glance.

Anon.

No one ever died from sleeping in an unmade bed. I have known mothers who remake the bed after their children do it because there is a wrinkle in the spread or the blanket is on crooked. This is sick.

Erma Bombeck

Housekeeping is like being caught in a revolving door.

Marcelene Cox

I buried a lot of my ironing in the backyard.

Phyllis Diller

I would rather lie on a sofa than sweep beneath it.

Shirley Conran

At worst, a house unkempt cannot be so distressing as a life unlived.

Rose Macauley

I'm eighteen years behind in my ironing. There's no use doing it now, it doesn't fit anybody I know.

Phyllis Diller

A Dirty Job, but Someone's Got to Do It!

People can say what they like about the eternal verities, love and truth and so on, but nothing's as eternal as the dishes.

Margaret Mahy

I will clean the house when Sears comes out with a riding vacuum cleaner.

Roseanne Barr

Few tasks are more like the torture of Sisyphus than housework, with its endless repetition: the clean becomes the soiled, the soiled is made clean, over and over, day after day.

Simone De Beauvoir

The important thing about women today is, as they get older, they still keep house. It's one reason why they don't die, but men die when they retire. Women just polish the teacups.

Margaret Mead

If your house is really a mess and a stranger comes to the door greet him with, 'Who could have done this? We have no enemies.'

Phyllis Diller

The worst thing about work in the house or home is that whatever you do is destroyed, laid waste or eaten within twenty-four hours.

Lady Hasluck

Mothers' Wit

Have you ever taken anything out of the clothes basket because it had become, relatively, the cleaner thing?

Katharine Whitehorn

Home is the girl's prison and the woman's workhouse.

George Bernard Shaw

Misery is when you make your bed and then your mother tells you it's the day she's changing the sheets.

Suzanne Heller

You can't get spoiled if you do your own ironing.

Meryl Streep

Laundry increases exponentially in the number of children.

Miriam Roberts

Now as always, the most automated appliance in a household is the mother.

Beverley Jones

A sparkling house is a fine thing if the children aren't robbed of their lustre in keeping it that way.

Marcelene Cox

Everybody wants to save the earth; nobody wants to help mom do the dishes.

P.J. O'Rourke

No one knows what her life expectancy is, but I have a horror of leaving this world and not having anyone in the entire family know how to replace a toilet tissue spindle.

Erma Bombeck

Behind every successful woman is a basket of dirty laundry.

Sally Forth

Famous Mums

I may be the only mother in America who knows exactly what their child is up to all the time.

Barbara Bush

I live for my sons. I would be lost without them.

Princess Diana

I've been chased through airports with a screaming baby because the photographers are ruthless, and they want the picture.

Lisa Marie Presley

I said I would get better with each baby, and I have.

Demi Moore

When you are a mother, you are never really alone in your thoughts. A mother always has to think twice, once for herself and once for her child.

Sophia Loren

Motherhood has a very humanizing effect. Everything gets reduced to essentials.

Meryl Streep

If you bungle raising your children, I don't think whatever else you do well matters very much.

Jacqueline Kennedy Onassis

All of a sudden I had a baby, because it went really quick. It was like, 'Oh! I have a baby!' So, it's great. I'm just having a great time with my children. They're here in New York with me.

Catherine Zeta-Jones

Motherhood is the strangest thing; it can be like being one's own Trojan horse.

Rebecca West

Since I had the baby I can't tolerate anything violent or sad, I saw *The Matrix* and I had my eyes closed through a lot of it, though I didn't need to. I would peek, and then think, 'Oh OK, I can see that.'

Lisa Kudrow

I love being with my children. They're fascinating people.

Amy Grant

I like playing mothers.

Dorothy Malone

I love acting but it's much more fun taking the kids to the zoo.

Nicole Kidman

I didn't worry about leaving the fast lane – I was just so consumed with my baby that it seemed like the right thing to do. I never felt like I left New York, though. If you've lived in a place and loved it, you never feel like you left it.

Sissy Spacek

I am proud that I am a good mother to my children, a good daughter to my mother, a good sister to my sis (Ashley Judd) and a good wife to my new husband.

Wynonna Judd

I fill myself up. I give myself 100 per cent to my children.

Janice Dickinson

You get to the stage when your children don't wake you up at six in the morning and can get on with stuff themselves.

Nigella Lawson

The world my children are growing up in is so much more sophisticated and exposed – emotionally, intellectually, sexually.

Amy Grant

I've told Billy if I ever caught him cheating, I wouldn't kill him because I love his children and they need a dad. But I would beat him up. I know where all of his sports injuries are.

Angelina Jolie

Mothers' Wit

You have to love your children unselfishly. That is hard. But it is the only way.

Barbara Bush

I'm a mother with two small children, so I don't take as much crap as I used to.

Pamela Anderson

As a mother, you feel much more vulnerable. And when you're vulnerable, you're a much better actress.

Kate Beckinsale

Grown don't mean nothing to a mother. A child is a child. They get bigger, older, but grown. In my heart it don't mean a thing.

Toni Morrison

Mum comes in and says 'I'm working out,' and she'll just be standing there naked doing a dance.

Kelly Osbourne

Motherhood has relaxed me in many ways. You learn to deal with crisis. I've become a juggler I suppose. It's all a big circus, and nobody who knows me believes I can manage, but sometimes I do.

Jane Seymour

I love being a mother ... I am more aware. I feel things on a deeper level. I have a kind of understanding about my body, about being a woman.

Shelley Long

Being a mother has made my life complete.

Darcy Bussell

Discovering that with every child, your heart grows bigger and stronger – that there is no limit to how much or how many people you can love, even though at times you feel as though you could burst – you don't – you just love even more.

Yasmin Le Bon

Children reinvent your world for you.

Susan Sarandon

Be a first-rate version of yourself, not a second-rate version of someone else.

Judy Garland, to her daughter, Liza Minnelli

There is nothing more thrilling in this world, I think, than having a child that is yours, and yet is mysteriously a stranger.

Agatha Christie

Then someone placed her in my arms. She looked up at me. The crying stopped. Her eyes melted through me, forging a connection in me with their soft heat.

Shirley Maclaine

When a child enters the world through you it alters everything on a psychic, psychological and purely practical level.

Jane Fonda

I love all my children, but some of them I don't like.

Lillian Carter, mother of President Jimmy Carter

As hard as nails on a crucifix.

Clive Barnes, referring to Mildred Dunnock's role as the mother in Days in the Trees

Because I am a mother, I am capable of being shocked: as I never was when I was not one.

Margaret Atwood

Don't call me an icon. I'm just a mother trying to help.

Princess Diana

First things first, second things never.

Shirley Conran

I was not a classic mother. But my kids were never palmed off to boarding school. So, I didn't bake cookies. You can buy cookies but you can't buy love.

Raquel Welch

The easiest way to convince my kids that they don't really need something is to get it for them.

Joan Collins

My father was frightened of his mother.

George V

I'm like old wine. They don't bring me out very often, but I'm well preserved.

Rose Kennedy, on her 100th birthday

Before I had a child I thought I knew all the boundaries of myself, that I understood the limits of my heart. It's extraordinary to have all those limits thrown out, to realize your love is inexhaustible.

Uma Thurman

I am not Superwoman. The reality of my daily life is that I'm juggling a lot of balls in the air … and sometimes some of the balls get dropped.

Cherie Blair

I want to spend more time with my family, but I'm not sure they want to spend more time with me.

Esther Rantzen

Once you become a mother, your heart is no longer yours … My daughter is the greatest thing I'll ever do in my life.

Kim Basinger

He's my wonderful, precious, little Buddha. He eats like a champion. He sleeps peacefully and he's the apple of his daddy's eye.

Sharon Stone

Maddox is my baby, he's by my side all the time, and I think I can give him so much. I can no more imagine living without him, than not breathing.

Angelina Jolie

The great high of winning Wimbledon lasts for about a week. You go down in the record book, but you don't have anything tangible to hold on to. But having a baby – there isn't any comparison.

Chris Everett Lloyd

I don't like waving my children like a celebrity trophy. I know everyone wants to see if they're fat and look like me.

Jo Brand

I have come, Sire, to complain of one of your subjects who has been so audacious as to kick me in the belly.

Marie Antoinette, telling Louis XVI of France that she was pregnant with their first child

Closing these two books, a reader senses that Joan Crawford, idol of an age, would have made an exemplary prison matron, possibly at Buchenwald. She had the requisite sadism, paranoia and taste for violence.

Harriet Van Horne, discussing Christina Crawford's writings about life with her adoptive mother, Joan Crawford

I'm very happy at home. I love to just hang out with my daughter, I love to work in my garden. I'm not a gaping hole of need.

Uma Thurman

I know I could really kill for my daughter … It's like, that's my lair and nobody messes with my lair.

Whitney Houston

Mick was against it at first but he's OK now. She made $60 000 in one week – what can you say?

Jerry Hall, discussing her daughter's modelling career

I had no experience with kids. I had no small brothers or sisters. I had to learn what to do with them. I had no idea when they walked, when they talked, when they got teeth.

Tracey Ullman

I've been through it all baby. I'm Mother Courage.

Elizabeth Taylor

I hope to leave my children a sense of empathy and pity and a will to right social wrongs.

Anita Roddick

Famous Daughters

It was no great tragedy being Judy Garland's daughter. I had tremendously interesting childhood years – except they had little to do with being a child.

Liza Minnelli

I wouldn't have turned out the way I was if I didn't have all those old-fashioned values to rebel against.

Madonna

It was pretty awful for us children because we never really knew the local children. Mother was keen for us to learn languages, so our travels took us to France and Italy, as well as the West Country.

Mary Wesley

Whenever my mother talks to me, she begins the conversation as if we were already in the middle of an argument.

Amy Tan

Is my mother my friend? I would have to say, first of all she is my Mother, with a capital 'M'; she's something sacred to me. I love her dearly … yes, she is also a good friend, someone I can talk openly with if I want to.

Sophia Loren

She tried in every way to understand me, and she succeeded. It was this deep, loving understanding as long as she lived that more than anything else helped and sustained me on my way to success.

Mae West

My mother's great. She has the major looks. She could stop you from doing anything, through a closed door even, with a single look. Without saying a word, she has that power to rip out your tonsils.

Whoopi Goldberg

The older I become, the more I think about my mother.

Ingmar Bergman

My mother phones daily to ask, 'Did you just try to reach me?' When I reply, 'No', she adds, 'So, if you're not too busy, call me while I'm still alive,' and hangs up.

Erma Bombeck

My mother used to say that there are no strangers, only friends you haven't met yet. She's now in a maximum-security twilight home in Australia.

Dame Edna Everage

I would have gone home to my mother, but I'm not that crazy about my mother.

Cher

Mum, have I sung at the Hollywood Bowl?

Charlotte Church

My mother taught me to walk proud and tall 'as if the world was mine'.

Sophia Loren

After my mother I never needed anyone else.

Mae West

When I was only about 5 or 6 years old, I was standing with my mother in the kitchen at home in Long Beach. I told her flat out that when I grew up I was going to be the best at something. She just smiled and kept peeling potatoes or whatever it was she was doing.

Billie Jean King

If God lets me live, I shall attain more than mummy ever has done, I shall not remain insignificant, I shall work in the world and for mankind!

Anne Frank

I ask people why they have deer heads on their walls. They say, 'Because it's such a beautiful animal.' There you go! I think my mother is attractive, but I have photographs of her.

Ellen DeGeneres

My mother and I could always look out the same window without ever seeing the same thing.

Gloria Swanson

What I object to in mother is that she wants me to think her thoughts. Apart from the question of hypocrisy, I prefer my own.

Margaret Deland

My playground was the theatre. I'd sit and watch my mother pretend for a living. As a young girl, that's pretty seductive

Gwyneth Paltrow

It has always frightened me that people should love her so much.

Queen Mother, of her daughter Elizabeth II as a child

My mother is Irish, my father is black and Venezuelan, and me – I'm tan, I guess.

Mariah Carey

I have a lot of people to thank, and I'm going to be one of those people that tries to mention a lot of names, because I know just two seconds ago my mother and father went completely berserk, and, uh, I'd like to give some other mothers and fathers that opportunity.

Meryl Streep, 55th Academy Awards

I'm still that little girl who lisped and sat in the back of the car and threw vegetables at the back of mum's head when we drove home from the market. That never goes.

Tracey Ullman

Aurora-Zebedee Naming Baby

I'm thinking about naming my first son Emmy so I can say I've got one. I want Emmy, Oscar and Tony – and my daughter Grammy.

Noah Wyle

I think my parents were high when they named me.

Jolene Blalock

My mother's very proud of the name she gave me. She thought it sounded rhythmically better. It doesn't really make a difference to me what people call me, but since my mother calls me Holly Marie when she's angry, I prefer just my first name.

Holly Marie Combs

Britney Spears says she plans to name her son London, because that's where her romance with Kevin Federline began. The couple were going to name the baby after where it was conceived, but it was too hard to say Olive Garden Bathroom Floor.

David Spade

My wife wanted to call our daughter Sue, but I felt in my family that was usually a verb.

Dennis Wolfgang

My mother is a botanist, she even named a flower after me. It's called the Bloomin' Idiot.

A.M. radio station

I want to name my kids after people I hate so I can beat them and feel good about it.

Anon.

One thing they never tell you about childraising is that for the rest of your life, at the drop of a hat, you will be expected to know your child's name and how old he or she is.

Erma Bombeck

Nanny Shenanigans

A babysitter is someone who watches your TV set while your kids cry themselves to sleep.

Anon.

Our sex life has been ruined since the arrival of our first baby. We can't be so spontaneous because we don't want the nanny to hear us. We can't scream and yell like we used to.

Cindy Crawford

I don't have a nanny or a housekeeper, and only have a cleaner for one hour each week. I finish work and go home. I cook the dinner. I run into Tesco and do the housework in the evening.

Victoria Beckham

There is possibly no guilt in this world to compare with leaving a sick child with a babysitter. The sitter could be Mother Theresa and you'd still feel rotten.

Erma Bombeck

A babysitter is a teenager acting like an adult whilst the adults are out acting like teenagers.

Anon.

She was a beautiful baby. She blew shining bubbles of sound. She loved motion, loved light, loved colour and music and textures. When she was just eight months old I had to leave her daytimes with the woman downstairs to whom she was no miracle at all.

Tille Olsen

I had a nanny who made me sit in front of a bowl of porridge for three or four days running when I refused to eat it. I remember being very unhappy about that.

Anjelica Huston

Mothers taken to the theatre when the kids are tiny, phone the sitter in the interval to see if they are alive and happy. Mothers taken to the theatre when the kids are in their teens phone home to see if it's still standing.

Peter Gray

I once spent more time writing a note of instructions to a babysitter than I did on my first book.

Erma Bombeck

The new childcare-screening legislation sends a powerful message to Americans: if you want to harass children, get your own, as no parent-screening legislation will be in the works any time soon.

Anon.

I should like the whole race of nurses to be abolished. Children should be with their mothers as much as possible in my opinion.

Lewis Carroll

Often, we expect too much [from a nanny]. We want someone like ourselves, bright, witty, responsible, loving, imaginative, patient, well-mannered and cheerful. Also, we want her to be smart, but not so smart that she's going to get bored in two months and leave us to go to medical school.

Louise Lague

An old timer remembers when babysitters were called mothers.

Anon.

P.I.M.s (Politically Incorrect Mothers)

Mothers' absence notes to their child's teacher:

Please excuse Jimmy for being. It was his father's fault.

Please excuse Jennifer for missing school yesterday. We forgot to get the Sunday paper off the porch, and when we found it Monday, we thought it was Sunday.

My daughter was absent yesterday because she was tired. She spent a weekend with the Marines.

Please excuse Mary for being absent yesterday. She was in bed with gramps.

Some mothers can trace their ancestors back three hundred years, but can't tell you where their children were last night.

Anon.

An ugly baby is a very nasty object – and the prettiest is frightful.

Queen Victoria

Children are the most desirable opponents at Scrabble as they are both easy to beat and fun to cheat.

Fran Lebowitz

I don't think my parents liked me. They put a live teddy bear in my crib.

Woody Allen

My mother had morning sickness after I was born.

Rodney Dangerfield

The lullaby is the spell whereby the mother attempts to transform herself back from an ogre to a saint.

James Fenton

I was a married woman and I had a baby. I would have adored it, but I just couldn't do it because I'm a lady.

Ruth Warrick

All God's children are not beautiful. Most of God's children are, in fact, barely presentable.

Fran Lebowitz

Young people especially have something invested in being nice people, and it's only when you have children that you realize you're not a nice person at all, but generally a selfish bully.

Fay Weldon

I've always been fascinated by the way that children and animals suffer stoically in a way that I don't think adults do.

Rebecca Miller

When I was a little kid we had a sand box. It was a quicksand box. I was an only child … eventually.

Stephen Wright

The peasants of the Asturias believe that in every litter of wolves there is one pup that is killed by the mother for fear that on growing up it would devour the other little ones.

Victor Hugo

I love my kids but I wouldn't want them for friends.

Janet Sorensen

There are no illegitimate children – only illegitimate parents.

Judge Leon R. Yankwich

Having children makes you no more a parent than having a piano makes you a pianist.

Michael Levine

I don't dislike babies, though I think very young ones rather disgusting.

Queen Victoria

And my parents finally realize that I'm kidnapped and they snap into action immediately: They rent out my room.

Woody Allen

Mothers' Wit

Children should be like waffles … you should be able to throw the first one away.

Nancy Mitford

My mother could make anybody feel guilty. She used to get letters of apology from people she didn't even know.

Joan Rivers

My mother never saw the irony in calling me a son-of-a-bitch.

Jack Nicholson

His mother should have thrown him away and kept the stork.

Mae West

I love children, especially when they cry, for then someone takes them away.

Nancy Mitford

He's a good boy; everything he steals he brings right home to his mother.

Fred Allen

My mother asked me to.

Marc Shreuder, when asked why he had murdered his grandfather

A mother! What are we worth really? They all grow up whether you look after them or not.

Christina Stead

P.I.M.s (Politically Incorrect Mothers)

Sometimes when I look at my children, I say to myself, 'Lillian, you should have remained a virgin.'

Lillian Carter (mother of President Jimmy Carter)

Do not join encounter groups. If you enjoy being made to feel inadequate, call your mother.

Liz Smith

They're all mine … Of course, I'd trade any one of them for a dishwasher.

Roseanne Barr

It would be better if they told their children, 'Go out and play in traffic.'

Dr Tazewell Banks, Director of Heart Program, DC General Hospital, commenting on mothers who feed their children fast food

The one regret I have about my own abortions is that they cost money that might otherwise have been spent on something more pleasurable, like taking the kids to movies and theme parks.

Barbara Ehrenreich

We all have bad days … one mother admitted leaving the grocery store without her kids – 'I just forgot them. The manager found them in the frozen food isle, eating Eskimo pies.'

Mary Kay Blakely

I can't ever remember being affectionate with my mother in a spontaneous way … I always had a sort of horror of her. When I dreamed of my mother when I was a little boy, she was either selling me or coming at me with a knife. The latter came true later on.

Jurgen Bartsch

My mother sent me to psychiatrists from the age of four because she didn't think little boys should be sad.

Andy Kaufman

I know what a mother tiger does when she's upset. She eats her young.

Guy Trosper and John Frankenheimer

When trouble comes no mother should have to plead guilty alone. The paediatricians, psychologists, therapists, goat herders, fathers, and peer groups should all be called to the bench as well …

Mary Kay Blakely

Women who cannot bear to be separated from their pet dogs, send their children to boarding schools quite cheerfully.

George Bernard Shaw

You know you've spent too much time car-pooling your kids when fast food drive-thru servers recognize your voice.

Linda Fiterman

I'd like to be the ideal mother, but I'm too busy raising my kids.

Anon.

LAWYER: How old is your son, the one living with you?
WITNESS: Thirty-eight or thirty-five, I can't remember which.
LAWYER: How long has he lived with you?
WITNESS: Forty-five years.

Genuine courtroom transcript

My mom said she learned how to swim. Her mother took her out in the lake and threw her off the boat. That's how she learned how to swim. I said, 'Mom, she wasn't trying to teach you how to swim.'

Paula Poundstone

Parents like the idea of kids, they just don't like their kids.

Morley Saefer

JACKIE (Patsy's sister): Our mother was like a sprinkler scattering bastard babies to the four corners of the earth.

Absolutely Fabulous

You're *Soooo* Embarrassing ...

Sing out loud in the car even, or especially, if it embarrasses your children.

Marilyn Penland

One time I ran out of the store and took the bus home by myself after my mother asked a salesclerk where the 'underpants' counter was. Everyone in the store heard her. I had no choice.

Phyllis Theroux

To my embarrassment I was born in bed with a woman.

Wilson Mizner

I've had young guys come on to me and I can't do it. I'm just not into it. I just can't do it … I wouldn't want to embarrass or humiliate my kids in any way.

Andie MacDowell

To a teenager there's nothing more embarrassing in the world than a mother.

Anon.

I was always embarrassed because my mother wore flat pumps and a cosy jumper, while my friend's mums were punks or hippies.

Shirley Manson

'Mummeeee, you forgot these!'

4-year-old child running down the aisle at Morrisons waving a packet of Tampax over her head – Anon.

Our 3-year-old daughter has developed a habit of shouting, 'loooook, it's dog poooooo!' at the top of her voice. Then she asks why it's brown and smelly and why we can't eat it.

Anon.

Mother's Ruin

Gin was mother's milk to her.

George Bernard Shaw

Seismic with laughter,
Gin and chicken helpless in her Irish hand

George Barker

Alcohol is a good preservative for everything but brains.

Mary Pettibone Poole

I remember when I was a kid I used to come home from Sunday school and my mother would get drunk and try to make pancakes.

George Carlin

I looked into that empty bottle and I saw myself.

Grace Metalious

My makeup wasn't smeared, I wasn't dishevelled, I behaved politely, and I never finished off a bottle, so how could I be alcoholic?

Betty Ford

Even though a number of people have tried, no one has yet found a way to drink for a living.

Jean Kerr

'My country, right or wrong', is a thing that no patriot would think of saying … It is like saying, 'My mother, drunk or sober.'

G. K. Chesterton

One reason I don't drink is that I want to know when I'm having a good time.

Nancy Astor

I like to have a martini,
Two at the very most –
At three I'm under the table,
At four I'm under the host.

Dorothy Parker

Alcohol doesn't solve any problems, but then again neither does milk.

Anon.

It's true love because if he said quit drinking martinis but I kept on drinking them and the next morning I couldn't get out of bed, he wouldn't tell me he told me.

Judith Viorst

Well, I knew Colin's mother / And let me tell you the truth / When she was nursing Colin / Her milk was 90 proof / She tried to kick the habit / She didn't know what to do / But if your baby looked like that / Then you'd be drinking too.

Chip Esten

They're trying to put warning labels on liquor saying, 'Caution, alcohol can be dangerous to pregnant women.' That's ironic. If it weren't for alcohol, most women wouldn't even be that way.

Anon.

Your Mother Should Know
Mothers' Advice and Words of Wisdom

I found out why cats drink out of the toilet. My mother told me it's because it's cold in there. And I'm like: how did my mother know that!

Wendy Leibman

There is so much to teach and time goes so fast.

Erma Bombeck

My mother said I must always be intolerant of ignorance but understanding of illiteracy. That some people, unable to go to school, were more educated and more intelligent than college professors.

Maya Angelou

Children's talent to endure stems from their ignorance of alternatives.

Maya Angelou

My mother always told me I wouldn't amount to anything because I procrastinate. I said, 'Just wait.'

Judy Tenuta

Hugs can do great amounts of good – especially for children.

Princess Diana

If you don't go to sleep, the tooth fairy mafia will pull out all your teeth and sell them on the black market.

Erma Bombeck

The biggest lesson we have to give our children is truth.

Goldie Hawn

Everybody today seems to be in such a terrible rush, anxious for greater developments and greater riches and so on, so that children have very little time for their parents. Parents have very little time for each other, and in the home begins the disruption of peace of the world.

Mother Theresa

My mother wanted me to understand that as a woman I could do pretty much whatever I wanted to, that I didn't have to use sex or sexuality to define myself.

Suzanne Vega

If you want a baby, have a new one. Don't baby the old one.

Jessamyn West

If you want children to keep their feet on the ground, put some responsibility on their shoulders.

Abigail Van Buren

Everyone is guilty at one time or another of throwing out questions that beg to be ignored, but mothers seem to have a market on the supply. 'Do you want a spanking or do you want to go to bed?' 'Don't you want to save some of the pizza for your brother?' 'Wasn't there any change?'

Erma Bombeck

I know how to do anything – I'm a mom.

Roseanne Barr

My mom used to say it doesn't matter how many kids you have … because one kid'll take up 100 per cent of your time so more kids can't possibly take up more than 100 per cent of your time.

Karen Brown

My mom told me you don't have to be popular or the prettiest. Just be who you are. Don't do what everyone else is doing. The last thing we need is more Stepford teens. It was great advice.

Anon.

When your mother asks, 'Do you want a piece of advice?' it is a mere formality. It doesn't matter if you answer yes or no. You're going to get it anyway.

Erma Bombeck

ARTHUR: It's at times like this I wish I'd listened to my mother.
FORD: Why, what did she say?
ARTHUR: I don't know, I never listened.

Douglas Adams

I thought she'd [her mother] offer me some sympathy. Instead she said, 'Don't you ever call me crying again! You wanted to be in this business, so you'd better toughen up.' And I did.

Jennifer Lopez

My momma always said life was like a box of chocolates … you never know what you're gonna get.

Forrest Gump

Mom always tells me to celebrate everyone's uniqueness. I like the way that sounds.

Hilary Duff

The bearing and the training of a child
Is woman's wisdom.

Lord Alfred Tennyson

Mother's words of wisdom: 'Answer me! Don't talk with food in your mouth!'

Erma Bombeck

At every step the child should be allowed to meet the real experience of life; the thorns should never be plucked from his roses.

Ellen Key

From birth to 18 a girl needs good parents; from 18 to 35, she needs good looks. From 35 to 55, good personality. From 55 on, she needs good cash. I'm saving my money.

Sophie Tucker

You wet the bed one more time and a rainbow will follow you around for the rest of your life.

Erma Bombeck

Mother always said that honesty was the best policy, and money isn't everything. She was wrong about other things too.

Gerald Barzan

My mother's best advice to me was: 'Whatever you decide to do in life, be sure that the joy of doing it does not depend upon the applause of others, because in the long run we are, all of us, alone.'

Ali MacGraw

The doctors told me that I would never walk, but my mother told me I would, so I believed my mother.

Wilma Rudolph, American athlete

As a child you never quite understood how your mom was able to know exactly what you were thinking … Sometimes mom would know what you were thinking before the thought entered your head. 'Don't even think about punching your brother,' she would warn before you had time to make a fist.

Linda Sunshine

Mother told me a couple of years ago, 'Sweetheart, settle down and marry a rich man.' I said, 'Mom, I am a rich man.'

Cher

Never have more children than you have car windows.

Erma Bombeck

My mother said it was simple to keep a man, you must be a maid in the living room, a cook in the kitchen and a whore in the bedroom. I said I'd hire the other two and take care of the bedroom bit.

Jerry Hall

Never say anything on the phone that you wouldn't want your mother to hear at your trial.

Sydney Biddle Barrows, offering advice to the women in her employ as escorts

Mother always told me my day was coming, but I never realized that I'd end up as the shortest knight of the year.

Gordon Richards, a jockey, referring to his knighthood

When you grow up your mother says, 'Wear rubbers or you'll catch cold.' When you become an adult you discover that you have the right not to wear rubbers and see if you catch cold or not. It's something like that.

Diane Arbus

Giving advice comes naturally to mothers. Advice is in the genes along with blue eyes and red hair.

Lois Wyse

When we as youngsters would accuse our mother of picking on us, her wise reply was, 'All you get from strangers is surface pleasantry or indifference. Only someone who loves you will criticize you.'

Judith Crist

Fearful as reality is, it is less fearful than evasions of reality … Look steadfastly into the slit, pinpointed malignant eyes of reality as an old-hand trainer dominates his wild beasts.

Caitlin Thomas

Dear Pete, Just a short note. Please don't do anything foolish. Seriously, Pete, please take care of yourself and don't be a hero. I don't need a Medal of Honor winner. I need a son. Love, Mom.

Mrs Mahoney to her son Lt Peter P. Mahoney, US Army, engraved on NY Vietnam War Memorial

Level with your child by being honest. Nobody spots a phony quicker than a child.

Mary MacCracken

Years ago my mother said to me, 'In this world, Elwood, you must be oh so smart or oh so pleasant.' For years I was smart. I recommend pleasant.

Elwood P. Dowd, Harvey

Make sure the lubricant is unscented. Don't join fashionable 'schools of thought'. Read everything."

Zadie Smith

For that's what a woman, a mother wants – to teach her children to take an interest in life. She knows it's safer for them to be interested in other people's happiness than to believe in their own.

Athenæus

Courage, her mother had once told her, was not simply the fact that you weren't scared of anything … it was being scared, and doing whatever it was anyway. Courage was dealing with your fears, and not letting them rule you.

Missy Good

Make sure you never, never argue at night. You just lose a good night's sleep, and you can't settle anything until morning anyway.

Rose Fitzgerald Kennedy

My mother says to look for a man who is kind. That's what I'll do. I'll find somebody who's kinda tall and handsome.

Carolyn, aged 8

My mother told me: 'You must decide whether you want to get married someday, or have a career.' … I set my sights on the career. I thought, what does any man really have to offer me?

Annie Elizabeth Delany, the second African American woman dentist licensed in New York State

Long as there's lunch counters, you can always find work.

The mother and aunts of Dorothy Allison, US waitresses

Every man has been brought up with the idea that decent women don't pop in and out of bed; he has always been told by his mother that 'nice girls don't'. He finds, of course, when he gets older that this may be untrue – but only in a certain section of society.

Barbara Cartland

… and moreover my mother told me as a boy (repeatedly) 'Ever to confess you're bored means you have no Inner Resources.' I conclude now I have no inner resources, because I am heavy bored.

John Berryman

My great-grandfather used to say to his wife, my great-grandmother, who in turn told her daughter, my grandmother, who repeated it to her daughter, my mother, who used to remind her daughter, my own sister, that to talk well and eloquently was a very great art, but that an equally great one was to know the right moment to stop.

Wolfgang Amadeus Mozart

Never play peek-a-boo with a child on a long plane trip. There's no end to the game. Finally I grabbed him by the bib and said, 'Look, it's always gonna be me!'

Rita Rudner

The best time to start giving your children money is when they will no longer eat it.

Barbara Coloroso

A child's fingers are not scalded by a piece of hot yam which his mother puts into his palm.

African proverb

Yes, I care about my kids' problems, and I long to make suggestions. But these days I wait for children to ask for help, and I give it sparingly.

Susan Ferraro

Mothers' Wit

I'll kill you, gal, if you don't stand up for yourself. Fight, and if you can't fight, kick; if you can't kick, then bite.

Cornelia, US slave, advising her daughter Fanny when they were both slaves in Tennessee

The toddler must say 'no' in order to find out who she is. The adolescent says 'no' to assert who she is not.

Louise J. Kaplan

Be a doctor! Be a lawyer! Be a leper missionary!

Diane Ladd, advising her daughter, Laura Dern, not to act

I wish you would moderate that fondness you have for your children. I do not mean you should abate any part of your care, or not do your duty to them in its utmost extent, but I would have you early prepare yourself for disappointments, which are heavy in proportion to their being surprising.

Mary Wortley

Mother always told me, if you tell a lie, always rehearse it. If it don't sound good to you, it won't sound good to no one else.

Leroy 'Satchel' Paige

Listen carefully to what country people call mother wit. In those homely sayings are couched the collective wisdom of generations.

Maya Angelou

It is not economical to go to bed early to save candles if the result is twins.

Anon.

My mother taught me to luxuriate in the place between where I am and where I want to be.

Anon.

Keep it simple. Make a blank face and the music and the story will fill it in.

Ingrid Bergman's advice to her daughter Isabella Rossellini about acting

Mother what is marrying? Spinning, bearing children and crying, daughter.

Spanish proverb

I remember telling my mother in high school I wanted to wait for the perfect girl. And she replied, 'Idiot! Even if you found her, she might be holding out for the perfect man.'

John Cage, Ally McBeal

She once told me that people are like snowflakes; every one special and unique … and in the morning you have to shovel 'em off the driveway.

Michael, describing his mother's advice in Queer as Folk

Well it doesn't matter how you feel inside, you know? It's what shows up on the surface that counts. That's what my mother taught me. Take all your bad feelings and push them down, all the way down, past your knees until you're almost walking on them. And then you'll fit in, and you'll be invited to parties, and boys will like you, and happiness will follow.

Marge, The Simpsons

My mama always used to tell me: if you can't find somethin' to live for, you best find somethin' to die for.

Tupac Shakur

Try to look at everything through the eyes of a child.

Ruth Draper

So I'm not Super Mum … Adjust!

Anon.

Give Me a Break!
High Days and Holidays

No self-respecting mother would run out of intimidations on the eve of a major holiday.

Erma Bombeck

I stopped believing in Santa Claus when my mother took me to see him in a department store, and he asked for my autograph.

Shirley Temple

Christmas, children, is not a date. It is a state of mind.

Mary Ellen Chase

On vacations: we hit the sunny beaches where we occupy ourselves keeping the sun off our skin, the salt water off our bodies, and the sand out of our belongings.

Erma Bombeck

Our children await Christmas presents like politicians getting in election returns: there's the Uncle Fred precinct and the Aunt Ruth district still to come in.

Marcelene Cox

By and large, mothers and housewives are the only workers who do not have regular time off. They are the great vacationless class.

Anne Morrow Lindbergh

Myths that need clarification: 'No matter how many times you see the Grand Canyon, you are still emotionally moved to tears.' False. It depends on how many children the out-of-towners brought with them who kicked the back of your seat from Phoenix to Flagstaff and got their gum caught in your hair.

Erma Bombeck

Christmas is a time when everybody wants his past forgotten and his present remembered. What I don't like about office Christmas parties is looking for a job the next day.

Phyllis Diller

A vacation frequently means that the family goes away for a rest, accompanied by mother, who sees that the others get it.

Marcelene Cox

Christmas … is not an eternal event at all, but a piece of one's home that one carries in one's heart.

Freya Stark

My mum used to say that Greek Easter was later because then you get stuff cheaper.

Amy Sedaris

It has long been my belief that in times of great stress, such as a four-day vacation, the thin veneer of family wears off almost at once, and we are revealed in our true personalities.

Shirley Jackson

Christmas is a race to see what gives out first, your money or your feet.

Anon.

Outings are so much more fun when we can savour them through the children's eyes.

Lawana Blackwell

Everyone has the right to go on holiday without the kids if they want to.

Laura Schlessinger

There is nothing sadder in this world than to awake Christmas morning and not be a child.

Erma Bombeck

You know, I love how kids of divorce really have the market cornered on family dysfunction, but let me share with you a typical Thanksgiving at the Turk household: it starts with my mother yelling at my sister for yelling at my grandmother who's yelling at the television screen, which happens to be the microwave.

Chris Turk, Scrubs

In America there are two classes of travel – first class, and with children.

Anon.

For one mother, joy is the quiet pleasure found in gently rubbing shampoo into her young child's hair. For another woman it's taking a long walk alone, while for yet another, it's revelling in a much anticipated vacation.

Eileen Stukane

For years my husband and I have advocated separate vacations. But the kids keep finding us.

Erma Bombeck

The Back of My Hand
Mothers and Discipline

Experts say you should never hit your children in anger. When is a good time? When you're feeling festive?

Roseanne Barr

By the time you are old enough to know that your parents were right, you have children of your own that think you are wrong.

Anon.

A little more matriarchy is what the world needs, and I know it. Period. Paragraph.

Dorothy Thompson

In every dispute between parent and child, both cannot be right, but they may be, and usually are, both wrong. It is this situation which gives family life its peculiar hysterical charm.

Issac Rosenfield

All children have to be deceived if they are to grow up without trauma.

Kazuo Ishiguro

Hotdogs always seem better out than at home; so do French fried potatoes; so do your children.

Mignon McLaughlin

If your kids are giving you a headache, follow the instructions on the aspirin bottle, especially the part that says 'Keep away from children.'

Susan Savannah

Remember, when they have a tantrum, don't have one of your own.

Dr Judith Kuriansky

If I raised my hand to wipe the hair out of my children's eyes, they'd flinch and call their attorney.

Erma Bombeck

The real menace about dealing with a 5-year-old is that in no time at all you begin to sound like a 5-year-old.

Jean Kerr

If a mute kid swears, should his mother wash his hands with soap?

Steven Wright

I'm going to stop punishing my children by saying, 'Never mind! I'll do it myself.'

Erma Bombeck

When my husband comes home, if the kids are still alive, I figure I've done my job.

Roseanne Barr

Parents should conduct their arguments in quiet respectful tones, but in a foreign language. You'd be surprised what an inducement that is to the education of children.

Judith Martin

If you raise three children who can knock out and hog tie a perfect stranger, you must be doing something right.

Marge, The Simpsons

The quickest way for a parent to get a child's attention is to sit down and look comfortable.

Lane Olinghouse

When my kids become wild and unruly, I use a nice, safe playpen. When they're finished I climb out.

Erma Bombeck

It is not a bad thing that children should occasionally, and politely, put parents in their place.

Colette

Some are kissing mothers and some are scolding mothers, but it is love just the same – and most mothers kiss and scold together.

Pearl S. Buck

Raising children is like chewing on a stone.

Arab proverb

All children behave as well as they are treated.

Jan Hunt

If a child annoys you, quiet him by brushing his hair. If this doesn't work, use the other side of the brush on the other end of the child.

Anon.

Children in a family are like flowers in a bouquet; there's always one determined to face in an opposite direction from the way the arranger desires.

Marcelene Cox

There are three ways to get something done: do it yourself, employ someone, or forbid your children to do it.

Monta Crane

If you set the example, you won't need to set many rules.

Mama Zigler

Discipline is a symbol of caring to a child. He needs guidance. If there is love, there is no such thing as being too tough with a child.

Bette Davis

No one in the world can take the place of your mother. Right or wrong, from her viewpoint you are always right. She may scold you for little things, but never for the big ones.

Harry S Truman

A young lady is a female child who has just done something dreadful.

Judith Martin

We spend the first twelve months of our children's lives teaching them to walk and talk and the next twelve telling them to sit down and shut up.

Phyllis Diller

Madam, there's no such thing as a tough child – if you parboil them first for seven hours, they always come out tender.

W.C. Fields

The whole concept of grounding children is utterly stupid – they just go off and rebel and don't like you. When my kids eventually come along, I don't want them not to like me.

Kate Winslet

When your mother is mad and asks you, 'Do I look stupid?' It's best not to answer her.

Megan, aged 13

If mum's not happy, nobody's happy.

Neeley, aged 13

Before becoming a mother I had a hundred theories on how to bring up children. Now I have seven children and only one theory: love them, especially when they least deserve to be loved.

Kate Samperi

Parenting is a negative thing. Keep your children from killing themselves, or anyone else, and hope for the best.

Erma Bombeck

As a parent you try to maintain a certain amount of control and so you have this tug-of-war … You have to learn when to let go. And that's not easy.

Aretha Franklin

Children and zip fasteners do not respond to force … except occasionally.

Katharine Whitehorn

Tired mothers find that spanking takes less time than reasoning and penetrates sooner to the seat of the memory.

Will Durant

I can remember the first time I had to go to sleep. Mom said, 'Steven, time to go to sleep.' I said, 'But I don't know how.' She said, 'It's real easy. Just go down to the end of tired and hang a left. So I went down the end of tired, and just out of curiosity I hung a right. My mother was there, and she said, "I thought I told you to go to sleep." '

Steven Wright

There are three main parenting jobs: getting your kid to go to sleep without bedtime problems, getting your kid to eat without being finicky, and getting your kid toilet trained. Nobody I know has scored three out of three.

Anon.

The hardest people to convince they are at retirement age are children at bedtime.

Shannon Fife

My grandfathers, my grandmothers and my mother hardly ever spanked at all. My grandfather said that if you spanked the little ones, you made them scared and they couldn't think.

Max Hanley

If I wanted a special doll, and I begged my mother for it, she would give me a speech about how I had three dolls at home and I didn't need another one, and … when she finished telling me why I shouldn't want what I wanted, I still wanted it just as badly – only I felt ashamed of myself for wanting it.

Nancy Samalin

The word no carries a lot more meaning when spoken by a parent who also knows how to say yes.

Joyce Maynard

If you want your children to turn out well, spend twice as much time with them, and half as much money.

Abigail Van Buren

What time I go to bed has zippo to do with what time you go to bed.

Susan Raffy (talking to her son)

You know you've lost control when you're the one who goes to your room.

Baba Bell Hajdusiewicz

An advantage to having one child is you always know who did it.

Baba Bell Hajdusiewicz

Children behave best when their stomachs are full and their bladders are empty.

Vicki Lansky

The other day I called my mother in desperation. 'I need help,' I said, 'I've used every threat on my kids you ever used on me and I've run out. Do you have anything stronger that you held out on me?'

Erma Bombeck

I don't believe in smacking children – I use a cattle prod.

Jenny Éclair

When my mom got really mad, she would say, 'Your butt is my meat.' Not a particularly attractive phrase. And I always wondered, 'Now, what wine goes with that?'

Paula Poundstone

Fathers on Mothers

The most important thing a father can do for his children is to love their mother.

Henry Ward Beecher

The impulse of the American woman to geld her husband and castrate her sons is very strong.

John Steinbeck

Ma-ma does everything for the baby, who responds by saying Da-da first.

Mignon McLaughlin

Where there is a mother in the home, matters go well.

Amos Bronson Alcott

No mother would ever willingly sacrifice her sons for territorial gain, for economic advantage, for ideology.

Ronald Reagan

I sincerely believe that if Bush and Cheney recognized the full humanity of other people's mothers around the world, they wouldn't commit the crimes they commit.

Wallace Shawn

You couldn't fool your mother on the foolingest day of your life if you had an electrified fooling machine.

Homer, The Simpsons

I can be a good father but I'm a terrible mother.

Rainier, Prince of Monaco

Mothers' Wit

A man's mother is his misfortune, but his wife is his fault.

Walter Bagehot

Sometimes my wife complains that she's overwhelmed with work and just can't take one of the kids, for example, to a piano lesson. I'll offer to do it for her, and then she'll say, 'No, I'll do it.' We have to negotiate how much I trespass into that mother role – it's not given up easily.

Anon.

Listen to your mother. Mothers are always right.

Brian Baldinger

It's not easy to juggle a pregnant wife and a troubled child, but somehow I manage to fit in eight hours of TV a day.

Homer, The Simpsons

Sue Ellen, you're a drunk, a tramp, and an unfit mother

J. R. Ewing, Dallas

It is impossible for any woman to love her children twenty-four hours a day.

Milton R. Sapirstein

Republicans understand the importance of bondage between a mother and child.

Dan Quayle

Mothers are the necessity of invention.

Bill Watterson

But a mother is like a broomstick or like the sun in the heavens ... whether the child is beaten by it or warmed and enlightened by it, it accepts it as a fact in nature.

George Bernard Shaw

Mothers on Fathers

When Charles first saw our child Mary, he said all the proper things for a new father. He looked upon the poor little red thing and blurted, 'She's more beautiful than the Brooklyn bridge.'

Helen Hayes

Women know more about life than men, especially when it comes to the children.

Angela Carter

Be a father. Your son has friends his own age; no boy needs a 44-year-old 'pal'.

Ann Landers

If it has tyres or testicles, you're going to have trouble with it.

Linda Furney

My mother thought of my father as half barbarian and half blunt instrument and she isolated him from his children.

Pat Conroy

My mom said the only reason men are alive is for lawn care and vehicle maintenance.

Tim Allen

EDINA: God, I hope you're not inviting that bloody, bullocky, selfish, two faced, chicken bastard, pig-dog man, are you?
SAFFY: You could just say 'dad'.

Absolutely Fabulous

No man is responsible for his father. That is entirely his mother's affair.

Margaret Turnball

Mother's Day

When you feel neglected, think of the female salmon who lays 3,000,000 eggs but no one remembers her on Mother's Day.

Sam Ewing

Don't forget Mother's Day. Or as they call it in Beverly Hills, Dad's Third Wife Day.

Jay Leno

No gift to your mother can ever equal her gift to you – life.

Anon.

Woman in the home has not yet lost her dignity, in spite of Mother's Day, with its offensive implication that our love needs an annual nudging, like our enthusiasm for the battle of Bunker Hill.

John Erskine

The only mothers it is safe to forget on Mother's Day are the good ones.

Mignon McLaughlin

There is nothing a mother likes better than breakfast in bed – cold toast, burned scrambled egg and a newly plucked rose dripping dew and greenfly into the cornflakes.

Peter Gray

She ain't my mother, so I ain't gonna get her nothin'.

Lee Trevino on a Mother's Day gift for his wife

A printed card means nothing except that you are too lazy to write to the woman who has done more for you than anyone in the world. And candy! You take a box to mother – and then eat most of it yourself!

Anna Jarvis

Spend at least one Mother's Day with your respective mothers before you decide on marriage. If a man gives his mother a gift certificate for a flu shot, dump him.

Erma Bombeck

Last year on Mother's Day the whole family got together for a big dinner and afterward, when mom started to clean up, I said to her, 'Don't bother with those dishes, mom. Today is Mother's Day, you can always do them tomorrow.'

Joey Adams

There will be other Mother's Days and a parade of gifts that will astound and amaze you, but not one of them will ever measure up to the sound of your children in the kitchen on Mother's Day whispering, 'Don't you dare bleed on mum's breakfast.'

Erma Bombeck

Mother of God

The real religion of the world comes from women much more than from men – from mothers most of all, who carry the key of our souls in their bosom.

Oliver Wendell Holmes

God could not be everywhere and therefore he made mothers.

Jewish proverb

An ounce of mother is worth a pound of clergy.

Spanish proverb

Mom, can we go Catholic so we can get communion wafers and booze?

Bart, The Simpsons

I regard no man as poor who has a godly mother.

Abraham Lincoln

The Vatican is against surrogate mothers. Good thing they didn't have that rule when Jesus was born.

Elayne Boosler

God will protect us, [my mother] often said to me. 'But to make sure,' she would add, 'carry a heavy club.'

Gypsy Rose Lee

I'm a godmother, that's a great thing to be, a godmother. She calls me god for short, that's cute, I taught her that.

Ellen DeGeneres

'Simon darling, I'm afraid you will have to speak to the children. I caught Tristram believing in God yesterday.'

The Trendy Ape, cartoon 1968

By the year 2000 we will, I hope, raise our children to believe in human potential, not God.

Gloria Steinem

A little girl became restless as the preacher's sermon dragged on and on. Finally, she leaned over to her mother and whispered, 'Mummy, if we give him the money now, will he let us go?'

Anon.

I hope my child will be a good Catholic like me.

Madonna

Every mother is like Moses. She does not enter the promised land. She prepares a world she will not see.

Pope Paul VI

When God thought of mother, He must have laughed with satisfaction, and framed it quickly – so rich, so deep, so divine, so full of soul, power, and beauty, was the conception.

Henry Ward Beecher

Pulling on Your Purse Strings

The odds of going to the store for a loaf of bread and coming out with *only* a loaf of bread are three billion to one.

Erma Bombeck

Shopping is better than sex. If you're not satisfied after shopping you can make an exchange for something you really like.

Adrienne Gusoff

Weekend planning is a prime time to apply the Deathbed Priority Test: on your deathbed, will you wish you'd spent more prime weekend hours grocery shopping or walking in the woods with your kids?

Louise Lague

My children dominated my buying habits and I knew it. They could sing beer commercials before their eyes could focus.

Erma Bombeck

Grocery shopping is so exciting! It's like unwrapping presents from yourself.

Marge, The Simpsons

I was in the supermarket the other day and I met a lady in the aisle where they keep the generic brands. Her name was 'woman'.

Steven Wright

A mother and her daughter grow closer every time every time they have a successful shopping spree. Shoes off, kettle on, loot divided. It dates back to the cave.

Samantha Armstrong

I was doing the family grocery shopping accompanied by two children, an event I hope to see included in the Olympics in the near future.

Anna Quindlen

Shopping is a woman thing. It's a contact sport like football. Women enjoy the scrimmage, the noisy crowds, the danger of being trampled to death, and the ecstasy of the purchase.

Erma Bombeck

I always say shopping is cheaper than a psychiatrist.

Tammy Faye Baker

I bet you deep down you still wish your mum would take you clothes shopping every August for the new school year.

Bridget Willford

Why would anyone steal a shopping cart? It's like stealing a 2-year-old.

Erma Bombeck

She was of the stuff of which great men's mothers are made. She was indispensable to high generation, hated at tea parties, feared in shops, and loved at crises.

Thomas Hardy

Shopping is probably the most underrated contact sport in the world.

Erma Bombeck

Mummy Dearest ...

Everything I am or ever hope to be, I owe to my angel mother.

Abraham Lincoln

A man loves his sweetheart the most, his wife the best, but his mother the longest.

Irish proverb

Whenever I'm with my mother, I feel as though I have to spend the whole time avoiding land mines.

Amy Tan

Food, love, career, and mothers, the four major guilt groups.

Cathy Guisewite

She was the archetypal selfless mother: living only for her children, sheltering them from the consequences of their actions – and in the end doing them irreparable harm.

Marcia Muller

I'm very loyal in relationships. Even when I go out with my mom I don't look at other moms.

Garry Shandling

A mother's love for her child is like nothing else in the world. It knows no law, no pity, it dares all things and crushes down remorselessly all that stands in its path.

Agatha Christie

Life began with waking up and loving my mother's face.

George Eliot

When I stopped seeing my mother with the eyes of a child, I saw the woman who helped me give birth to myself.

Nancy Friday

All women become like their mothers. That is their tragedy. No man does. That's his.

Oscar Wilde

My mother was the most beautiful woman I ever saw. All I am I owe to my mother. I attribute all my success in life to the moral, intellectual and physical education I received from her.

George Washington

Mother love is the fuel that enables a normal human being to do the impossible.

Marion C. Garretty

If the whole world were put into one scale, and my mother in the other, the whole world would kick the beam.

Henry Bickersteth

Mother – that was the bank where we deposited all our hurts and worries.

T. DeWitt Talmage

Whatever else is unsure in this stinking dunghill of a world a mother's love is not.

James Joyce

Who ran to help me when I fell, And would some pretty story tell, Or kiss the place to make it well? My mother.

Ann Taylor

To describe my mother would be to write about a hurricane in its perfect power.

Maya Angelou

We only have one mom, one mummy, one mother in this world, one life. Don't wait for the tomorrow to tell mum you love her.

Anon.

In the beginning there was my mother. A shape.
A shape and a force, standing in the light.
You could see her energy; it was visible in the air.
Against any background she stood out.

Marilyn Krysl

I am old enough to be – in fact I am – your mother.

A.A. Milne

My mother lived the latter years of her life in the horrible suspicion that electricity was dripping invisibly all over the house.

James Thurber

Yes, mother. I can see you are flawed. You have not hidden it. That is your greatest gift to me.

Alice Walker

Nobody loves me but my mother, and she could be jivin' too.

B. B. King

My mother is jelly-hearted and she has a brain of jelly:
Sweet, quiver-soft, irrelevant. Not essential.
Only a habit would cry if she should die ...

Gwendolyn Brooks

My mother wanted to shrink from my clinging, but did not.

Mason Cooley

My mother read secondarily for information; she sank as a hedonist into novels. She read Dickens in the spirit in which she would have eloped with him.

Eudora Welty

I love my mother for all the times she said absolutely nothing.

Erma Bombeck

So I begin to understand why my mother's radar is so sensitive to criticism. She still treads the well-worn ruts of her youth, when her impression of mother was of a woman hard to please, frequently negative, and rarely satisfied with anyone – least of all herself.

Melinda M. Marshall

A slight digression: that bit about my mother was a deliberate lie. In reality, she was a woman of the people, simple and coarse, sordidly dressed in a kind of blouse hanging loose at the waist.

Vladimir Nabokov

I realized that, while I would never be my mother nor have her life, the lesson she had left me was that it was possible to love and care for a man and still have at your core a strength so great that you never even needed to put it on display.

Anna Quindlen

Health Issues

The best medicine in the world is a mother's kiss.

Anon.

My father invented a cure for which there was no disease and unfortunately my mother contracted it and died of it.

Victor Borge

The mother is not dying exactly, but has reached a point in life where death is a familiar on the staircase.

Clive Barnes, commenting on Days in the Trees

A smart mother makes often a better diagnosis than a poor doctor.

August Bier

Why, Madam, do you know there are upward of thirty yards of bowels squeezed underneath that girdle of your daughter's? Go home and cut it; let Nature have fair play, and you will have no need of my advice.

John Abernethy, a surgeon speaking to a mother who had brought her tightly laced daughter for treatment

You'll have to excuse my mother. She suffered a slight stroke a few years ago which rendered her totally annoying.

Dorothy, The Golden Girls

Patient has two teenage children but no other abnormalities.

Written on a patient's medical charts

A woman came to ask the doctor if a woman should have children after 35. I said 35 children is enough for any woman!

Gracie Allen

Kids on Mums

To choose the right mom for your kids you got to find somebody who likes the right stuff. Like if you like sports she should keep the chips and dip coming.

Alan, aged 10

If nobody got married there sure would be a lot of kids to explain, wouldn't there?

Kelvin, aged 8

You gotta tell your mom that she looks pretty even if she looks like a truck.

Ricky, aged 10

If it's your mother, you can kiss her any time. But if it's a new person, you have to ask permission.

Roger, aged 6

God makes mothers out of clouds and angel hair and everything nice in the world – and one dab of mean.

Anon.

Mom doesn't want to be boss, but she has to because dad's such a goofball.

Anon.

Moms know how to talk to teachers without scaring them.

Anon.

The greatest mom in the world wouldn't make me kiss my fat aunts!

Anon.

Her teeth are perfect, but she bought them from the dentist.

Anon.

If your sister hits you, don't hit her back. Your mum always catches the second person.

Paula, aged 9

When my mum is mad at my dad, I don't let her brush my hair.

Louisa, aged 6

Never tell your mum her diet's not working.

Joel, aged 14

From Cradle to Grave

My mother's love is the almond blossom of my mind and the fragrance is worth dying for. Her gentle compassionate touch shaped my very essence and – forever – I shall remember and although we are separated by the corridor of life and the door way of heaven, I will always attempt to become the man that she perceived me to be.

Frank L. de Roos III

There she was in her bed. Dead. But nobody explained it to me. They told me later that she had gone to America.

Vartan Gregorian, describing his mother's death when he was aged 7

'Jakie, is it my birthday or am I dying?'
Her son replied, 'A bit of both, Mum.'

Viscountess Nancy Astor, on her deathbed

Mother died today. Or perhaps it was yesterday, I don't know.

Albert Camus

The mother is everything – she is our consolation in sorrow, our hope in misery, and our strength in weakness. She is the source of love, mercy, sympathy, and forgiveness. He who loses his mother loses a pure soul who blesses and guards him constantly.

Kahlil Gibran

There I sat, in the biting wind, wishing she were gone.

Krapp, speaking of his dying mother, in Samuel Beckett's Krapp's Last Tape

The death of a mother is the first sorrow wept without her.

Anon.

'What is your mother's maiden name?'; what's her first name, I just knew her as 'Ma'! That'll have to do. (writing on the form) 'Ma. Possibly deceased.'

Bernard, Black Books

I may be dead, but I'm still your mother.

Nicky Silver, Raised in Captivity

'Poor Clifton … is still, after two months, wailing and sobbing over Mabelle's death. As she was well over 90, gaga, and driving him mad for years, this seems excessive and over indulgent … It must be tough to be orphaned at 71!'

Noël Coward, discussing Clifton Webb's distress at the death of his elderly mother

I went into the kitchen and got halfway to the phone before I realized that I couldn't call her … A lot of people who lost a mother or father or husband or wife will tell you that they find themselves almost talking out loud. I do that a lot.

Bill Clinton, following his mother's death

Index

Index

Index

Index

Index

Index